Labor Law, Industrial Relat
and
Employee Choice

The State of the Workplace in the 1990s

Hearings of the Commission on the
Future of Worker-Management Relations, 1993-94

Richard N. Block
John Beck
Daniel H. Kruger
Michigan State University

1996

W.E. Upjohn Institute for Employment Research
Kalamazoo, Michigan

Library of Congress Cataloging-in-Publication Data

Block, Richard N.
    Labor law, industrial relations, and employee choice : the state of the workplace in
the 1990s : hearings of the Commission on the Future of Worker-Management
Relations, 1993-94 / Richard N. Block, John Beck, Daniel H. Kruger.
        p. cm.
    Includes bibliographical references and index.
    ISBN 0–88099–163–1 (paper : alk. paper). — ISBN 0–88099–164–X (cloth : alk.
paper)
    1. Labor laws and legislation—United States.   2. Industrial relations—United
States.   I. Beck, John, 1954-   . II. Kruger, Daniel H.   III. United
States.   Commission on the Future of Worker-Management Relations.   IV. Title.
KF3369.849   1996
344.73'01—dc20   96–26103
[347.3041]   CIP

The facts presented in this study and the observations and viewpoints expressed are
the sole responsibility of the authors. They do not necessarily represent positions of
the W. E. Upjohn Institute for Employment Research.

Cover design by J. R. Underhill
Index prepared by Shirley Kessel.
Printed in the United States of America.

Dedication

To Henry and Ferne Block, Ann Austin-Beck, and Carol Beals

Special Dedication

To Gerald Alan Block, Public Defender
June 1, 1952 – March 14, 1996
who dedicated his life to fairness for all

The Authors

Richard Norman Block is professor of labor and industrial relations at Michigan State University. He is the author of numerous articles and books on such issues as the relationship between law and practice in industrial relations, industrial relations and structural economic change, employment law, and employee training. He is an experienced labor-management neutral currently listed on all major arbitrator rosters, as well as the panel on matters related to the implementation of the North American Agreement on Labor Cooperation, and the labor aids agreement of North American Free Trade Agreement. Professor Block received his B.S. and M.S. degrees in economics from the University of Illinois at Urbana-Champaign and his Ph.D. in labor and industrial relations from Cornell University.

John P. Beck is assistant professor in the School of Labor and Industrial Relations at Michigan State University since 1991. He works primarily in two of the School's research units, the Labor Education Program and the Project on Innovative Employment Relations Systems (PIERS). He is the author of a number of articles on labor history, technological change, and workplace innovation. Prior to joining the staff of the School, he spent five years as education and research director of the United Paperworkers International Union, devoting much of his time to the Union's efforts in the areas of joint labor-management cooperation and workplace innovation. He received his B.A. from Michigan State University and M.A. from the University of Michigan.

Daniel H. Kruger is a professor of industrial relations at Michigan State University where he has been on the faculty since 1957. He received his B.A. from the University of Richmond and his M.A. and Ph.D. from the University of Wisconsin. He has served extensively as a fact finder and an arbitrator in both the private and public sectors. He has written numerous articles for professional journals in the area of human resources, collective bargaining, grievance administration, and arbitration. In 1992 President Bush reappointed him for an unprecedented third five-year term on the Federal Service Impasses Panel.

Preface

The Commission on the Future of Worker-Management Relations (the Dunlop Commission) met for one of its regional hearings in East Lansing, Michigan on the campus of Michigan State University on October 13, 1993. The interaction and discussion between the commissioners and the presenters formed the original inspiration and rationale for this volume. The breadth of experience presented and the quality of dialogue convinced the authors that something more needed to be done regarding the hearings, beyond the final report that the Commission was charged to deliver.

Since commissions of this type have been rare in U.S. history, the Dunlop Commission provided a unique opportunity for today's analysts and practitioners to take stock of the current practice of labor-management relations. We decided to start the important process, which other contemporary researchers and future historians might follow, of using the hearing testimony as an important primary document for research and analysis. This is of key importance, since the testimony covered a broader range of experiences, and with richer detail and deeper exploration, than the Commission was able to give proper attention in its report. (In fact, this volume has no relation to the Commission report and should be viewed as distinct from it.)

In the East Lansing hearings, for example, the Commissioners and the audience were not only treated to some of the examples of cooperative and adversarial labor relations chronicled in this book, but also heard presentations on grievance mediation, disability management, workplace diversity, employment-at-will, and other important workplace issues as well. Though we could not and did not cover all the presentations in this volume (we did read every one of them!), we invite other scholars and practitioners to go to the source and see for themselves the wealth of material embedded in the Commission testimony.

We would like to thank all of those connected to the East Lansing hearings who piqued our interest enough to initiate this project, including Douglas Fraser, Thomas Kochan, and Paula Voos, the Commissioners who came to East Lansing to hear testimony, and M. Peter McPherson, president of Michigan State University and Randall Eberts, executive director of W.E. Upjohn Institute for Employment Research, who represented the sponsoring organizations. The East Lansing hearings would not have been possible without the following corporations, unions, and individuals who gave testimony: Miller Brewing and United Autoworkers Local 2308, Trenton, Ohio; Herman Miller Company; Donnelly Corporation; Johnson Controls and the International

Association of Machinists Lodge 66, Milwaukee, Wisconsin; Mead Paper and United Paperworkers International Union Local 21, Escanaba, Michigan; Dow Chemical; International Business Machines; General Motors; Service Employees International Union, District 1199, Columbus, Ohio; United Food and Commercial Workers Local 951, Grand Rapids, Michigan; Graphic Communications International Union Local 577M, West Allis, Wisconsin; Amalgamated Clothing and Textile Workers Union, Findlay, Ohio; the United Autoworkers International Union; Varnum, Riddering, Schmidt and Howlett; Professor Rochelle Habeck; and Professor Theodore St. Antoine.

CONTENTS

Labor Law, Industrial Relations and Employee Choice

CHAPTER **1**

Introduction and Overview

The past two decades of industrial relations experience have had the cumulative effect of a widespread realization that discussion and debate over the nation's labor laws and their administration are needed. Concerns have been growing about the costs to society of labor conflict, and questions have been raised as to whether there is a role for labor legislation in encouraging labor-management cooperation in order to enhance the global competitiveness of U.S. firms.

In response to this accumulation of concerns, the Secretaries of Commerce and Labor in 1993 created the Commission on the Future of Worker-Management Relations, often referred to as the Dunlop Commission, as it was chaired by former U.S. Secretary of Labor John Dunlop. The task of the Commission was to investigate the current state of worker-management relations and labor law and make recommendations concerning changes that may be needed to improve productivity through increased worker-management cooperation and employee participation in the workplace.

A widely diverse set of experiences was presented as public testimony before the Commission in 1994. Representatives of labor, management, government, academia, and the general public presented a picture of considerable variation in current labor relations practice. The whole of this testimony, however, pointed to the need for a continued public discourse about labor law, and quite possibly, the need for fundamental change. Labor law, as it has been developed since the Wagner Act in 1935, has always been based on the concept of the parties—individual workers, unions, and management—making choices. The Dunlop Commission hearings pointed up a new range of choices being explored by workers and managers and the frustration of some of the traditional choices originally designed into the law.

We believe that the Dunlop Commission hearings recorded the dominant issues in industrial relations today, and that the testimony offers a unique opportunity to understand the state of labor-management relations in the United States in the 1990s. The purpose of this book is to capture the essence of the hearings and make it accessible to the industrial relations community, to policy makers, and to the general public.

Historical Background

Union membership in the United States has shown great historical variation. Membership rose fairly steadily between 1897 and 1904, as the internal structure of the movement attained some stability with the advent of the American Federation of Labor. Strong business conditions also led to an increase in the power of union membership. Eventually, unionization reached a high of about 12 percent of the nonagricultural labor force in 1904, and remained at about 11 percent through 1916. World War I and its aftermath increased the rate to about 19 percent by 1921. Boom business conditions brought about by the war and government policy to encourage labor peace had much to do with the success of unions during this period (Block and Premack 1983; Troy 1965).

The 1920s were a decade of decline for unions due to the recession of 1920-1923, employer welfare capitalism in the middle 1920s, postwar government pressure on left-wing activities emanating from the Russian Revolution, and the onset of the depression. Unionization reached a post-World War I low point of 10.7 percent in 1930. The early New Deal legislation that provided some support for unionization was associated with a slight increase in the rate of unionization, to about 13.3 percent in 1935 (Block and Premack 1983; Troy 1965).

The passage of the Wagner Act in 1935 was clearly associated with a significant increase in unionization. Between 1935 and 1941, the unionization rate increased 10 points, to 23 percent of the labor force. Another significant increase was associated with World War II. By the end of the war, unionization had increased to about 30 percent of the labor force. During the war, the encouragement to unionization provided by the Wagner Act was augmented by the pro-collective bargaining policies of the War Labor Board, designed to avoid strikes that would disrupt the war effort (Troy 1965; "Termination Report of the National War Labor Board" 1947; Taylor 1948; Witte 1946).

Small increases in unionization continued after the war through the early 1950s. The rate of unionization peaked at approximately 35 percent in 1955. Since then, unionization has steadily declined. In 1995, approximately 16.5 percent of the U.S. labor force was represented by unions. A somewhat deeper examination shows that this rate is propped up by the high rate of unionization (43.5 percent) in the public sector. Private sector unionization was at about 11.4 percent, comparable to the level of unionization in the mid-1920s, when there was no legislation in the United States protecting workers' rights to organize. The decline in unionization from 1955-1994 is unprecedented in the United States, and shows no signs of abating (Troy 1965; Meltz 1990; Chaison and Rose 1991; *Daily Labor Report* No. 28, 1992, pp. B-1 to B 5; U.S. Department of Labor 1996).

Indeed, the United States ranked 22 out of 24 OECD countries in the rate of unionization in 1988, with a unionization rate of 16.8 percent. Only Spain, at 16 percent, and France at 12.8 percent ranked below the United States in the OECD study. By contrast, major U.S. competitors such as Canada, Germany, and Japan had unionization rates of 34.6 percent, 33.8 percent, and 26.8 percent, respectively (OECD 1991).

As a result of this long-term decline in unionization, the United States is in one of those critical periods in its history when ferment in the industrial relations community suggests that it may be time to reexamine industrial relations institutions. The first such critical period was 1933-47. During this fifteen-year period, an economic depression and widespread strike activity resulted in the passage of the National Labor Relations (Wagner) Act, which was designed to create a system for peacefully determining whether employees wished to be represented by a union and to raise the standard of living of workers by allowing them to bargain collectively with their employer.

During that period, labor and management, with the intervention of the World War II War Labor Board, established many of the industrial relations mechanism and principles that are still in use. However, employers continued to advocate for changes in the Wagner Act that they contended would bring balance into the industrial relations system. This pressure, in combination with a rash of strikes in 1946, resulted in the passage of the Taft-Hartley Act of 1947 over the veto of President Harry Truman.

The thirty-year period following Taft-Hartley was one of overall stability in industrial relations. By the late 1940s, collective bargaining was well-established, especially in the manufacturing and transportation industries. Moreover, these industries exhibited remarkable economic prosperity. With little foreign competition, manufacturing continued to generate large profits and high standards of living for workers. Regulation generally prevented the entry of nonunion competitors and permitted price stability in transportation, a situation that resulted in high wages for unionized workers and high profits for employers.

As noted, however, hidden under this stability were some trends that suggested the industrial relations system was moving towards a crisis. Private sector unionization rates began a steady decline from a high of roughly 35 percent in the mid 1950s. Interpretations of the National Labor Relations Act by the courts and the National Labor Relations Board were making it increasingly difficult for unions to organize (see chapter 2). By the late 1970s, an increasingly competitive economic environment was causing management to question the established practices within industrial relations. While some firms responded to changes in the competitive environment by cooperating with unions, others engaged in conflict, attempting to eliminate unions representing their employees.

Since the late 1970s, unions have experienced increasing difficulties within the industrial relations system. Although the economic environment has no doubt been responsible for part of the decline in the fortunes of unions, it has become increasingly clear, first to unionists and then to many neutral observers, that the nation's labor law is a major contributing factor. While private sector industrial relations in the United States is affected by many phenomena, labor law is likely the factor that affects it most directly. The law applies to all of the parties, whereas the effect of economic conditions can vary from firm to firm. In addition, the law contains compulsion—once one party invokes its procedures, the other party must go along. Third, the law is very public and open to all. Legal decisions are reported, and attorneys are very aware of them. Thus, these decisions can be used to argue for or against future conduct in labor relations.

Just as employers became concerned about the state of industrial relations in the late 1930s and early 1940s—concerns that were reflected in the Taft-Hartley Act—unions have also developed legislative initiatives to address their concerns.

In 1976-77, the AFL-CIO spearheaded an unsuccessful campaign for labor law reform. The Labor Law Reform Act of 1977 failed to survive a filibuster in the U. S. Senate in the face of strong business opposition to the legislation's attempt to speed up the election process and increase penalties on parties found in violation of labor laws.[1]

A second union-supported initiative to change the nation's labor laws started in 1989 when legislation was proposed to end the use of permanent replacement workers during labor disputes. First introduced as a bar to the use of replacements for the first ten weeks of a strike, the legislation was reintroduced as a flat ban in 1990. The legislative history on this issue came to an abrupt end in July of 1994 with two failed cloture votes in the U. S. Senate. Thus, the measure died, although it had passed the House of Representatives with a wide majority in 1993 and would have been signed by President Clinton (*Daily Labor Report*, various issues).

Just as unions had bitterly opposed the Taft-Hartley changes in the late 1940s, employers opposed the labor law changes of the late 1970s and early 1980s. The difference, however, is that employers were successful in their opposition, while unions were unsuccessful.

Commission on the Future of Worker-Management Relations

The Commission on the Future of Worker-Management Relations was created in March 1993 in response to an accumulation of concerns. There were growing fears that the nation's labor laws were neither adequately addressing the rights of employees to organize and bargain collectively, nor supporting the emerging structures and understandings being built in both union and nonunion workplaces to advance employee voice and satisfaction.

The creation of such a commission is a rare event. This is only the second governmental commission appointed in this century to take a broad-based look at employment relations in the United States; the

United States Commission on Industrial Relations was established in 1912 and issued its final report in 1915. In addition, in 1947 the National Planning Association appointed the Committee on the Causes of Industrial Peace to undertake case studies of cooperative collective bargaining relationships. An excerpt from the final reports of each of these two bodies demonstrates the ongoing nature of many of the comments and concerns highlighted in this volume.

Excerpt from the Final Report of the U. S. Commission on Industrial Relations (1915):

> A more serious and fundamental charge is, however, contained in the allegation by the workers that in spite of the nominal legal rights which have been established by a century long struggle, almost insurmountable obstacles are placed in the way of their using the only means by which economic and political justice can be secured, namely combined action through voluntary organization....
>
> As a result, therefore, not only of fundamental considerations but of practical investigations, the results of which are described in detail hereinafter, it would appear that every means should be used to extend and strengthen organizations through the entire industrial field. Much attention has been devoted to the means by which this can best be accomplished, and a large number of suggestions have been received. As a result of careful consideration, it is suggested that the commission recommend the following action:
>
> 1. Incorporation among the rights guaranteed by the Constitution of the unlimited right of individuals to form associations, not for the sake of profit but for the advancement of their individual and collective interests.
>
> 2. Enactment of statues specifically protecting this right and prohibiting the discharge of any person because of his membership in a labor organization.
>
> 3. Enactment of a statute providing that action on the part of an association of individuals not organized for profit shall not be held to be unlawful where such action would not be unlawful in the case of an individual.
>
> 4. That the Federal Trade Commission be specifically empowered and directed by Congress, in determining unfair methods of competition to take into account and specially investigate the

unfair treatment of labor in all respects, with particular reference to the following points:

(a)Refusal to permit employees to become members of labor organizations.

(b)Refusal to meet or confer with the authorized representatives of employees.

5. That the Department of Labor, through the Secretary of Labor or any other authorized official, be empowered and directed to present to the Federal Trade Commission, and to prosecute before that body all cases of unfair competition arising out of the treatment of labor which may come to its attention.

6. That such cases, affecting as they do the lives of citizens in the humblest circumstances, as well as the profits of competitors and the peace of the community, be directed by Congress to have precedence over all other cases before the Federal Trade Commission.[2]

Excerpt from the Final Report of the Committee on the Causes of Industrial Peace:

In the Committee's statements introducing each "Case Study" some basic causes of industrial peace have been listed. The list has varied and been expanded as the studies accumulated. It has one distinguishing characteristic. Each cause on the list refers to attitudes and approaches which the parties themselves have consciously adopted or helped to achieve. Furthermore, each was important in explaining the degree of industrial peace found in the specific case. It is worth repeating the complete list here.

1. There is full acceptance by management of the collective bargaining process and of unionism as an institution. The company considers a strong union an asset to management.

2. The union fully accepts private ownership and operation of the industry; it recognizes that the welfare of its members depends upon the successful operation of the business.

3. The union is strong, responsible, and democratic.

4. The company stays out of the union's internal affairs; it does not seek to alienate the workers' allegiance to their union.

5. Mutual trust and confidence exist between the parties. There have been no serious ideological incompatibilities.

6. Neither party to bargaining has adopted a legalistic approach to the solution of problems in the relationship.

7. Negotiations are problem-centered—more time is spent on day-to-day problems than on defining abstract principles.

8. There is widespread union-management consultation and highly developed information sharing.

9. Grievances are settled promptly, in the local plant whenever possible. There is flexibility and informality within the procedure.[3]

Between May 1993 and April 1994, the Commission on the Future of Worker-Management Relations (the Dunlop Commission) held eleven national hearings and six regional hearings. The national hearings were held in Washington, D.C. The six regional hearings were held in Louisville, East Lansing (Michigan), Atlanta, San Jose (California), Houston, and Boston. Those testifying included representatives from all strata of the industrial relations community: corporate CEOs, international union presidents, corporate human resources officials, plant managers, first-line supervisors, regional and local union officials, union organizers, and hourly workers, both unionized and non-union. The result was a true cross-section of day-to-day industrial relations life in the United States that only a governmental body with the status of a national commission could assemble.

This volume differs from the Commission's "Fact-Finding Report" and "Report and Recommendations" in two fundamental ways. First, although we would hope that this volume will inform the policy debate on the law of labor-management relations, it is not designed to put forth detailed policy recommendations, which was the mission of the Commission.

Second, as in most documents designed to create policy recommendations, the Commission in its "Fact-Finding Report" and "Report and Recommendations" was only able to briefly summarize and highlight the evidence and testimony that form the basis of its recommendations. It was our view that the details of this evidence represented a rare window into the variation that was thought to exist in labor-management relations in the United States. A policy-oriented summary did not do it justice. The purpose of this volume is to do what the Commission could not do—make the richness of that testimony available in an organized, accessible format to the business, labor, and policy communities in the United States.

This book does not address all possible issues arising under labor law. Most notably, it does not address unfair and illegal tactics by unions during organizing drives. No evidence of such tactics was brought before the Commission. While such actions by unions may occur, the absence of any strong movement to amend Section 8(b) of the National Labor Relations Act (the provisions creating union unfair labor practices), suggests that the current provisions in the NLRA regulating union behavior in organizing campaigns are serving their intended purpose.

This effort was undertaken with the knowledge of the Commission. In order to maintain the independence of the authors and of the Commission, no member of the Commission had any involvement in the preparation or review of the manuscript. The book is the sole responsibility of the authors and does not necessarily reflect the views of the Commission on the Future of Worker-Management Relations, the W.E. Upjohn Institute for Employment Research, or the Michigan State University School of Labor and Industrial Relations.

Chapter 2 of the book will place the subsequent chapters in their legal, historical, economic, and industrial context, demonstrating that the essence of the industrial relations system is the protection of employee choice to be represented by a union, or not to be represented by a union. Specifically, chapter 2 will discuss how the U.S. industrial relations system can produce wide variation in employment relations practices revolving around the matter of employee choice. Chapter 3, based on the transcripts of the hearings, will focus on innovative employment relationships in which employers respect employee choice, both to be represented by a union and to choose to remain non-union. Chapter 4, also based on the transcripts, discusses some examples of how the law permits employers to interfere with and infringe upon employee choice. Chapter 5 will discuss some conclusions and policy implications.

NOTES

1. The story of the Labor Law Reform Act of 1977-78 is chronicled in issues of the *Daily Labor Report* for that time period.

2. *Final Report of and Testimony Submitted to Congress by the Commission on Industrial Relations Created by the Act of August 23, 1912*, Vol. I, Washington, DC: Government Printing Office, 1915, especially pp. 61, 67-68.

3. *Causes of Industrial Peace Under Collective Bargaining*, Clinton S. Golden and Virginia D. Parker, eds., New York: Harper & Bros., 1955, p. 47.

CHAPTER 2

Labor and Industrial Relations Law and Practice in the United States

Overview of Labor and Industrial Relations Law

The basic law covering union-management relations in the United States is the National Labor Relations Act (NLRA), first enacted in 1935. Sweeping amendments were adopted in 1947, with additional amendments enacted in 1959 and 1974. The latter amendments brought private, nonprofit health care institutions under the coverage of the NLRA. Although one can summarize some of the basic principles of the NLRA fairly quickly, an important aspect of this chapter is the history of the law and how it evolved.[1]

The National Labor Relations (Wagner) Act of 1935

The NLRA (Wagner Act) was passed in 1935, on the heels of widespread strike activity that occurred in 1934. The ostensible reasons for passage of the NLRA, as found in the preamble to the law, were to avoid the disruption of commerce caused by strikes over the recognition of unions and to permit employees to exercise their collective bargaining power to raise living standards (Bernstein 1969, ch. 4-7; Keyserling 1945, pp. 5-33). Thus, Section 1, under "Findings and Policies" stated:

> The denial by employers of the right of employees to organize and the refusal by employers to accept the procedure of collective bargaining led to strikes and other forms of industrial strife or unrest, which have the intent or the necessary effect of burdening or obstructing commerce . . ..

> The inequality of bargaining power between employees who do
> not possess full freedom of association or actual liberty of con-
> tract, and employers who are organized in the corporate or other
> forms of ownership association substantially burdens and affects
> the flow of commerce, and tends to aggravate recurrent business
> depressions, by depressing wage rates and the purchasing power
> of wage earnings in industry and by preventing the stabilization of
> competitive wage rates and working conditions within and
> between industries.

Later in the statute, in Section 7, the rights of employees to engage
in collective activity were made explicit:

> (e)mployees shall have the right to self-organization to form, join,
> or assist labor organizations, to bargain collectively through repre-
> sentatives of their own choosing, and to engage in concerted activ-
> ities for the purpose of collective bargaining or other mutual aid or
> protection.

As such, the purpose of the NLRA was to provide a peaceful means
for determining whether a group of employees chose to be represented
for collective bargaining purposes by a labor organization. To effectuate the employee choice process for unionization and to guarantee
employees their Section 7 rights, the NLRA created employer unfair
labor practices, making unlawful some employer practices that were
thought to prevent employees from exercising their rights. Declared
unlawful were such specific practices as discriminating against or discharging an employee for exercising rights given by the NLRA, giving
testimony or filing a charge under the NLRA, and dominating or interfering with the formation of a labor organization. The NLRA also
established a general prohibition, making it an unfair labor practice for
employers to "interfere with, restrain, or coerce" employees in the
exercise of their rights. In including this latter unfair labor practice,
Congress acknowledged that it could not anticipate all the various
ways in which employers could interfere with the rights of employees.

The Wagner Act also made it an unfair labor practice for an
employer to refuse to bargain collectively with the union chosen by its
employees. Thus, the Wagner Act provided the employees the opportunity to realize the fruits of their choice by imposing an obligation on
the employer to bargain with the union, if chosen.

The rights under the Act would be worth little if they could not be enforced. To that end, the Wagner Act also created a three-member National Labor Relations Board (NLRB), a specialized administrative agency, the sole function of which was to administer the NLRA. As the wording in the NLRA was purposefully broad, the NLRB, like other administrative agencies to be created, would actually legislate, by making substantive legal decisions regarding what employers were permitted, and were not permitted, to do. Board members were appointed by the president and confirmed by the Senate, and served staggered, five-year terms. Thus, although the Board was supposedly neutral in matters of labor relations, its political composition would change with the shifting political consensus (Bernstein 1969, p. 326).

The Board had (and continues to have) two major tasks; to determine whether an "appropriate unit" of employees wished to be represented by a union (the "representation" function), and to prevent unfair labor practices (the "enforcement" function). The representation issue contains two questions: is the unit (group of employees) for which the union is seeking representation appropriate, and if so do those employees wish to be represented by a union? For a unit to be appropriate, the Board examined whether there were sufficient common work interests among a group of employees such that they could form a cohesive bargaining unit. Such factors as similar skills, similar wage rates, similar job duties, comparable supervision, and geographic proximity are considered in these determinations.[2]

In determining whether a unit of employees wished to be represented by a union, the Board initially matched the signatures on union authorization cards with employer payroll records. If a majority of the employees had signed authorization cards, the Board would certify the union as the employees' bargaining representative. By the mid-1940s, however, the Board had developed the representation election as an alternative to card checks.[3]

In addition to its representation role, the Board was empowered to investigate and prevent unfair labor practices. If a complaint was filed, the Board was required to give all parties due process through notice of hearing, the right to respond, and the right to appear in person and give testimony. Board decisions could be enforced by the courts of appeals, and a party "aggrieved" by a Board decision could appeal the decision to the courts of appeals. A right to request Supreme Court review was also included.

Finally, the Wagner Act contained certain exclusions from coverage. Employers excluded were those who were too small to "affect commerce," public employers, nonprofit hospitals, and railroads and airlines, as those industries were already covered by the Railway Labor Act enacted in 1926. Employees excluded were agricultural workers, domestics, and employees of parents or spouses.

The Labor-Management Relations (Taft-Hartley) Act of 1947

Employer opposition to the Wagner Act culminated in passage of the Taft-Hartley Act of 1947. Taft-Hartley addressed employer concerns that the Wagner Act was one-sided. It amended Section 7 to make employees' rights to refrain from union activity a right comparable to employees' rights to engage in union activity. It created a series of union unfair labor practices, prohibiting unions from restraining or coercing employees and employers, from refusing to bargain, and from engaging in secondary activity (defined as union pressure on the employees of a neutral employer to encourage those employees to cease work where the purpose of the pressure is encouraging the neutral to "cease doing business" with the primary employer). It excluded supervisors from the law's coverage. Hoping to speed up the Board's processes, it increased the size of the NLRB from three to five members, while permitting the Board to delegate its authority to three-member panels. It also outlawed the closed shop (except in the construction industry), gave employers the right of free speech, made the certification election the preferred method of determining representation, and permitted states to enact legislation prohibiting companies and unions from requiring union membership as a condition of employment.

The Labor-Management Reporting and Disclosure (Landrum-Griffin) Act of 1959

The LMRDA filled some loopholes in the secondary activity provisions of Taft-Hartley and placed limits on recognitional and organizational picketing by unions. The major purpose of Landrum-Griffin, however, was to regulate the internal affairs of unions. It created stringent requirements on the internal governance of unions and provided legal protection for the rights of members within their unions.

Health Care Amendments of 1974

The Health Care Amendments of 1974 brought nonprofit hospitals and health care institutions under the jurisdiction of the NLRA in order to eliminate the disruptions to patient care caused by recognitional strikes in health care institutions. This concern about strikes also resulted in the Health Care amendments creating additional dispute resolution machinery to reduce the possibility of a strike in a health care institution over the negotiation of a collective agreement.[4]

Interpretation of the Law

The NLRB and the courts have generated thousands of pages of doctrinal law on the various provisions of the National Labor Relations Act. This section of the chapter will give a sense of the evolution and substance of those doctrines.

Workers Rights to Self-Organization and Concerted Activity

It is important to understand that the Wagner Act, and its successors, gave very few rights to unions. Rather, rights were conferred upon *employees*. Employees had the right to choose to unionize or not through the right of self-organization, the right to engage in concerted activity for mutual aid and protection, and the right to form, join, and assist a labor organization. Taft-Hartley gave employees the right to refrain from such activity. The employer unfair labor practices in the law are designed to prevent employers from infringing on these rights. Although the union unfair labor practices are somewhat more extensive than the employer unfair labor practices, they are mainly designed to prevent unions from infringing on employee rights and to minimize the extent to which a union may involve neutrals in labor disputes.

Starting in the spring of 1937, after the constitutionality of the Wagner Act was upheld,[5] the Board made decisions that became standard labor law doctrine. Discharge for union activity, employer domination and assistance to a labor organization, and outright refusal to bargain all violated the express language of the Act and were declared unlawful. Using Section 8(1), the general language prohibiting employer interference, restraint, and coercion, the NLRB declared unlawful many of the most notorious practices of employers, such as industrial espionage, the hiring of provocateurs, and private police (Bernstein 1969, pp. 648-50).[6]

Although actions that involved obvious antiunion motivation were, not surprisingly, unlawful, the Board was also willing to look beyond motivation to inferred effects on employee choice, regardless of employer motivation. In the 1945 case of *Republic Aviation Corp.* v. *NLRB* and *NLRB* v. *LeTourneau*, the Supreme Court upheld a Board decision finding the employer in violation of the NLRA for prohibiting employees from wearing union buttons, soliciting for a union on non-work time (breaks, lunch hours) on the property, and distributing prounion literature in the employer's parking lot. Although conceding that the employers had not demonstrated overt antiunion animus (the union button prohibition was adopted pursuant to its policy of remaining neutral in labor matters, the no-solicitation rule was designed to maintain an orderly workplace, and the no-distribution rule was designed to prevent littering), the Court upheld a Board ruling that the workplace was uniquely appropriate for organizing, and some dislocation of the employer's property rights was acceptable if it facilitated employee rights under the Wagner Act.[7]

Board decisions, however, were subject to appeal to the courts of appeals, and review by the Supreme Court. Subject to such oversight, Board decisions were not always upheld. Such was the situation in the Board doctrine that employers could not be involved in the process of unionization. The Board rule was based on the principle that anything the employer said during the process of unionization was inherently coercive, given the employees' dependence on the employer. Moreover, the Board believed that the unionization decision was solely that of the employees; the employer had no right to be involved in it. In 1941, the Supreme Court rejected this view in *NLRB* v. *Virginia Electric and Power Co.*, in essence saying that a Board finding that an employer committed an unfair labor practice based solely on the employer's, noncoercive, nonthreatening speech infringed on the employer's constitutional free speech rights.[8]

Virginia Electric and Power marked a watershed in labor law doctrine. It signaled that the employer need not remain neutral during the unionization process. Although employers were not permitted to threaten, restrain, or coerce employees, they could give their opinions of unions and collective bargaining (Block and Wolkinson 1986, pp. 43-82).

Employer rights in campaigns were extended further under the "captive audience" doctrine. An employer delivers a captive audience speech when it directs employees to assemble during working hours and listen to its views on unionization. The Board in 1942 had found the delivery of a captive audience speech unlawful, as the forced attendance was associated with a strong inference of employee dependence on the employer. Such a doctrine, however, was viewed by the courts as an unacceptable infringement on the employer's property rights. In 1947, a court of appeals held that the employer could deliver such a speech, provided it gave the union a similar opportunity. In 1954, the Board ruled that the employer generally could deliver a captive audience speech without giving the union the opportunity to respond so long as the speech was delivered more than twenty-four hours prior to the representation. The Board did not believe that the union was placed at a disadvantage by using the traditional means of contacting employees, such as in-plant solicitation, house calls, union meetings, and distribution of literature.[9]

Virginia Electric and Power and later cases reinforced substantial employer involvement in the unionization process during working hours. Employee involvement, however, was limited to nonworking hours and efforts away from the premises.[10]

In 1956, in *Babcock and Wilcox Company* v. *NLRB*, the Supreme Court overturned a Board decision and ruled that the employer did not violate the Labor Relations Act when it prohibited nonemployee union organizers from entering the employer's property to solicit for unionization. In essence, the Court ruled that *nonemployee union organizers*, as distinct from *employees exercising rights of self-organization*, were comparable to trespassers, and that they were not permitted on the property unless the employees were inaccessible and the union had no other reasonable means away from the employer's premises to contact the employees.[11]

The practical effect of *Babcock and Wilcox* would only become clear after the Board and the Courts had interpreted the term "reasonable." Over the next thirty years, the courts, generally overturning Board decisions, placed a heavy burden on unions to demonstrate that employees were "inaccessible" away from the workplace so that they would be permitted on the employer's premises. By the mid-1980s the law had evolved to the point where employees would be viewed as accessible away from the workplace and the employer's property if the employees ever left the employer's property, even if only for short periods of time. Thus, employees of barge lines who live and work on the barges and whose time spent off of the barges was intermittent and of short duration were considered accessible away from the workplace. Only in cases involving worksites in the Alaskan wilderness where employees *never* left the employer's property for weeks at a time were the employees found to be inaccessible away from the employer's property such that union access to the property for organizing was permitted. This principle that employees would be considered accessible to the union if they ever left the employer's premises was affirmed by the U.S. Supreme Court in 1992.[12]

This discussion of the evolution of labor law and the law of union organizing suggests that by the mid-1960s employers had at their disposal a set of tools to resist union organizing that they did not possess in the late 1930s; in essence, employer tactics that were illegal in the early Wagner Act years had become legal. By 1941, employers could campaign against the union at the workplace. Between 1942 and 1954, employers obtained the right to assemble their employees and deliver captive audience speeches without giving the union the same opportunity. By the late 1960s, employers had obtained the right to keep nonemployee organizers off of their property.

By 1970, employers had almost total control over the organizing campaign at the workplace, the place where employees congregated. During working hours employers could campaign as intensively as they wished, gathering employees in small and large groups to deliver an antiunion, albeit noncoercive message. They could generally prevent the union from coming on the premises to present its point of view, relegating the union to house visits, leaflets, and other voluntary measures. Nonunion employers who were determined to resist unions now had the means to do so.

Given this evolution in the law, it would be expected that the percentage of elections in which employees choose union representation would decline. This is precisely what has happened consistently since 1942.[13]

Employers' Duty to Bargain

The Wagner Act made it an unfair labor practice for an employer to refuse to bargain with the representative of its employees, which the Board interpreted as an obligation to bargain in good faith. This obligation was a derivative of the employees' right to choose unionization. This right would be of little value if there were no corresponding obligation on the part of the employer to honor that choice.

The Wagner Act provided the Board with little guidance on the definition of the phrase "to bargain." Taft-Hartley, however, added some meat to one sentence in the Wagner Act. It amended the NLRA by stating that the employer and the union had the obligation to "meet at reasonable times and confer in good faith with respect to wages, hours, and other terms or conditions of employment" but that this obligation did "not compel either party to agree to a proposal or require the making of a concession."[14]

The message from Taft-Hartley is that the obligation to bargain was to be primarily procedural. The parties were obligated to meet and to discuss terms and conditions of employment, but neither side was obligated to agree to anything. As the Supreme Court noted in the seminal *Insurance Agents* case:

> ... the nature of the duty to bargain in good faith thus imposed on employers by (Section) (8)(5) was not sweepingly conceived. The Chairman of the Senate Committee declared: "When the employees have chosen their representatives, all the bill proposes to do is to escort them to the door of their employer and say,'Here they are, the legal representatives of your employees.' What happens behind those doors is not inquired into, and the bill does not seek to inquire into it.

> ...It is apparent from the legislative history of the whole Act that the policy of Congress is to impose a mutual duty upon the parties to confer in good faith with a desire to reach an agreement, in the belief that such an approach from both sides of the table promotes

the over-all design of achieving industrial peace. . . . But apart from this essential standard of conduct, Congress intended that the parties should have wide latitude in their negotiations, unrestricted by any governmental power to regulate the substantive solution of their differences.[15]

Thus an important policy decision under the Act is that the Board is not to be involved in the substance of bargaining, and may not act so as to equalize bargaining power. The bargain between the employer and the union must reflect the relative bargaining power, interests, and wishes of the parties. Outcomes of bargaining are not subject to governmental intervention. Similarly, government may not affect the outcomes of bargaining indirectly by adjusting (equalizing) the bargaining power of the parties.[16]

There is no inconsistency between the existence of good-faith bargaining, on the one hand, and the use of bargaining weapons for "self-help" purposes on the other. Thus, a union may strike, a classic tactic which is designed to inflict harm on the employer. When a union strikes, it is hoping that the employer's loss of business will force it to concede to the union's proposals before the loss of income to the union and its members force them to concede to the employer's proposals. But an employer, under the self-help principle, may hire permanent replacements for strikers so as to try and keep its business going. Alternatively, an employer may determine the timing of a work stoppage by locking out the employees.

By the mid-1940s, a second important issue had begun to evolve: the scope of bargaining, e.g., about what issues must the parties bargain, and what issues could be addressed unilaterally by the employer? (Millis and Brown 1950, p. 117). As Taft-Hartley limited bargaining to "terms and conditions and employment," in 1958, the Supreme Court ruled the parties were only obligated to negotiate over "mandatory subjects of bargaining," e.g., terms and conditions of employment. Matters not falling within the definition of "terms and conditions of employment" were "permissive," with either side having the legal authority to refuse to bargain over those issues. If the parties were to be permitted to use economic weapons (strikes, lockouts), the impasse must be over only mandatory subjects.[17]

This "mandatory-permissive distinction" generated litigation as to whether certain employer decisions were not negotiable because they were not terms and conditions of employment and, therefore, not mandatory subjects of bargaining. Generally, employers would attempt to exclude items from the scope of bargaining, while unions would attempt to include them. The distinction became a major issue in the 1960s in cases involving major employer business and capital allocation decisions that also had an effect on employment. Were such decisions terms and conditions of employment because they normally involved the loss of jobs, or were they nonmandatory subjects of bargaining because they involved decisions fundamental to the direction of the enterprise that were related to traditional notions of managerial control? Over a period of almost thirty years, from 1964 to 1993, the Board and the courts, including the Supreme Court on two separate occasions, resolved the issue. The Board, relying on a 1981 Supreme Court decision in *First National Maintenance*, accepted the principle that decisions representing a basic change in the nature of the business were not mandatory subjects of bargaining. In general, an employer must bargain over a work relocation or capital investment decision only if there is no basic change in the nature of the business and if labor costs are such an important factor in the decision that it is possible that the union could have offered sufficient concessions to change the decision.[18]

Although the mandatory-permissive distinction as it has evolved is quite consistent with traditional U.S. notions of property rights, it has created conflict between employers and unions over the scope of negotiations. Rather then encouraging the parties to work together to resolve their problems, the *First National Maintenance* doctrine has provided a vehicle for employers to shift product and make capital investment, and by implication, employment decisions, without consulting with the union (Sockell 1986, pp 19-34; Block and Wolkinson 1989, pp. 2005-2056).

Case Processing Time

Generally, the Board administers the Act expeditiously. Between 1970 and 1990, it took the Board (actually the Board's regional director) roughly forty-two days to issue a decision in representation (election) cases, with an election generally scheduled for roughly thirty days thereafter. Moreover, about 94 percent of unfair labor practice cases are resolved informally, either with a dismissal, a withdrawal, or a settlement (NLRB *Annual Reports,* 1976-91).

Because the Board is a quasi-judicial agency, however, parties before the Board have certain procedural rights they may exercise. In a representation case, an employer may challenge the union's definition of a bargaining unit, contending it includes classifications that do not have a community of interest with other employees in the proposed bargaining unit or excludes classifications that do have a community of interest. Such a challenge, however, will result in an adversary hearing before a Board administrative law judge if it is not resolved informally. The losing party in the election may object to the results based on the behavior of the other party during the preelection period. This challenge is generally based on the questionable campaign tactics of the winning party.

Processing time for unfair labor practice charges can also be extended by a refusal of either party to settle the case. If no settlement is forthcoming, the case will go before an administrative law judge, who will issue a recommended order. This recommended order will either be affirmed, modified, or rejected by the Board. Both sides have the right to take the case to the court of appeals. There is also a right to request review from the Supreme Court. Thus, resolution of an unfair labor practice case, if all procedural rights are exercised, can take several years.

Even if one assumes that exercise of the legal rights is done in good faith, the process does result in delay in resolving cases. Delay in resolving NLRB cases not only harms the aggrieved party (usually an employee), assuming that party ultimately prevails, it also may change the industrial relations outcomes of Board cases.

For example, in election cases, the normal two-month time period between a union request for an election and the election itself tends to favor employers, as they can use their greater access to the employee-voters to influence undecided voters to vote against union representation. Since the average union election is decided by only eight votes, small increases in time are important. While it may be that this decline in union support is the result of employees' receiving information during the campaign, voter turnout also declines with delay; one would think that more information would cause participation to increase

(Roomkin and Block 1981, pp. 75-97; Block, Wolkinson and Kuhn 1988; Block 1990b, pp. 145-153).

Challenging the bargaining unit also results in delay. The employer may use the period during which the unit issue is being considered to campaign against unionization, using the tools that it has developed. Data indicate that employer success in elections increases when there is a challenge to the union's requested bargaining unit.[19]

Delay in unfair labor practice proceedings, through appeals, can have three effects. First, it puts off the remedy due to the employees. If the employee has been unlawfully discharged or demoted, the result is a loss of income, and possibly benefits (if the employee has been unlawfully discharged). Second, appeals can change the outcome of a case. While employers have the option of settling an unfair labor practice charge, a recent study indicated that an employer taking an unfair labor practice case as far as it can stands an 83 percent chance of an ultimately favorable decision. Thus, it is not surprising that one-third of all cases that result in a finding of an unfair labor practice by the Board (usually an employer violation) are closed with a court order rather than a Board decision. While this may indicate that the employer did not violate the Act, such cases almost always involve the workplace rights of the parties and are often value-laden industrial relations issues. They rarely involve issues that involve the existence of the business. Such judicial behavior in overruling the Board tends to reduce the authority of the Board and overlegalize the industrial relations system (Block 1994, pp. 250-259; Block and Roomkin 1995).

Finally, the processing time for an unfair labor practice case affects a related representation case. Normally, the Board will not conduct an election while an unfair labor practice is pending, on the grounds that its remedy will dissipate the election effects of the unfair labor practice if the employer is found in violation of the Act.

Remedies

Because the NLRB is an administrative agency and not a court, remedies under the NLRA are designed to be remedial rather than punitive. To the extent possible, the Board, through its remedies, attempts to re-create the situation prior to the commission of the unfair labor practice. It has no authority to punish the violator.

Under the remedial scheme of the NLRA, discharged employees are returned to the position they would have held had they not been discharged, with back pay plus interest, less interim earnings. In principle, this returns the employee to the situation in which he or she found him or herself prior to the unfair labor practice. But the unlawfully discharged employee may be left without a remedy for several years if the employer exhausts all appeals. It has been argued that such a remedial scheme encourages employers to discharge employees for the effect of the discharge on other employees. For the employer who is so inclined, the cost of back pay may be much less than the cost of a union, if the employer is able to discourage union activity and allegiance through the discharge.[20]

A second remedial principle is that the Board may not impose a substantive term on either party. In refusal to bargain cases, this means that the only order the Board can issue is a cease-and-desist order, in essence a directive that the employer stop refusing to bargain. During the interim, while the case is being heard and decided, a process that can take many months, the employees are without a contract. This is one of the major reasons why only about 75 percent of certifications result in a first contract.[21]

The Law and Industrial Relations

This brief overview of major NLRA doctrinal and procedural issues indicates how that law has evolved in ways that have given employers the legal tools to vigorously resist unions if they so choose. They have been able to use case processing time to resist union organizing at the workplace, and they have been able to use the mandatory-permissive distinction to limit the scope of union involvement where unions represent employees. A nonpunitive remedial scheme has provided an incentive system that encourages employers who are so inclined to disregard the spirit or the letter of the law and intimidate or coerce employees who might wish to exercise their right to self-organization. While it is true that most employers probably do not use the legal system to prevent employee self-organization, the important point is that it can be used that way if an employer wishes. It is these aspects of the legal system that have caused many of the problems that surfaced in the hearings.

Equally important, however, although somewhat less obvious than doctrine, are the basic principles underlying industrial relations policy in the United States. This country has opted for minimal government involvement in the labor relations system. As regards organizing, this means that there are few constraints on the workplace behavior of the employer, provided that it does not otherwise violate the rights of employees. As regards collective bargaining with an established union, the government is not to be involved in determining the terms and conditions of employment.

The bargaining process is to determine outcomes based on the preferences of the parties, the ideology of the parties, and the relative power of the parties pursuant to the self-help principle. Thus, our collective bargaining policy permits parties to behave very well towards each other, or very poorly towards each other. Alternatively, one party can behave poorly and the other well. As will be seen, this system results in a wide range of behaviors and labor relationships.[22]

Industrial Relations since World War II

This legal overview examines the employment relations system that has developed since World War II. This section will first provide an overview of the unionized employment relations system, followed by a discussion of the nonunion employment relations system.

The Unionized Employment Relations System

An understanding of the unionized employment relations system in the United States can best be obtained by taking an historical perspective. From the mid-1930s through the early 1980s, there was a single dominant model for labor-management relations. It has been called the New Deal model of industrial relations, and it can be described as institutionalized adversarialism.

Features of Adversarialism

Under the New Deal system of institutionalized adversarialism, each party recognized the institutional legitimacy of the other, with neither attempting to eliminate the other. The union wanted the company to prosper, and it attempted to insure that employees share in that prosperity. The company, although recognizing the union as the legitimate representative of its employees, attempted to limit the union's effectiveness in achieving employee gains, hoping to retain more of the company's surplus for the shareholders.

Not only did both sides recognize each other's institutional legitimacy, each side also recognized that the other had a role to play in the system. The union recognized that it was the company's role to manage the enterprise: to decide what to produce, how to produce it, and determine such matters as staffing, pricing, and work organization. The union generally had no interest in becoming involved in these decisions. Its role was to represent the employees on matters related to employment, and to protest if it believed that a management decision violated the agreement or the law.

Neither party had any interest in becoming involved in the institutional prerogatives of the other. The company generally opposed such union involvement; and the union, as the representative of the employees, was often reluctant to be involved, preferring to protest a management decision rather than accept the political consequences of being involved in making management decisions that might be viewed as contrary to the interests of workers.

The parties generally negotiated collective agreements that were detailed and highly legalistic. They dealt with such matters as institutional security, compensation, working conditions, and seniority. Almost all contained a grievance procedure that ended in final and binding arbitration to resolve disputes. Consistent with the mandatory-permissive distinction, collective agreements tended to be detailed documents that limited rights of management in areas related to terms and conditions of employment, but generally gave management wide latitude in other areas.

Communication was highly structured into two distinct channels: contract negotiations and the grievance procedure. During contract negotiations, which occurred generally every two to three years, the parties determined the terms of the collective bargaining agreement, generally modifying the former agreement. Once the agreement was signed, union-management communications usually were conducted through the grievance procedure, generally a means of protesting management decisions through a grievance alleging that the employer had violated the agreement. In almost all cases, an allegation that the contract had been violated generated a formal grievance, which was processed through two or three layers of union and management. Grievances that could not be resolved were submitted to binding arbitration, a quasi-legal process before a neutral selected by a procedure agreed to by the parties in their labor agreement.

The system of institutionalized adversarialism, although cumbersome and legalistic, proved satisfactory to both parties at least through the mid-1970s. It met the union's need for institutional security and for a formal role in representing the employees. At the same time, it limited union involvement to issues involving terms and conditions of employment, and provided an acceptable means for resolving disputes over these matters, generally leaving management free to make business decisions at the strategic level.

While protecting the institutional interests of each party, this system tended to be inflexible. The legalistic, fixed-duration contracts could not be modified to accommodate changed conditions unless both parties agreed. The rigid job structures and seniority systems in many agreements, designed to prevent management from using favoritism and arbitrariness in assigning jobs or laying off employees, also made it difficult for firms to reallocate workers to more productive uses as the need arose.

Despite these inherent difficulties, the economic prosperity during the postwar period provided an appropriate environment for such a system. Product markets sheltered from competition provided strong profits which, in turn, permitted growing employment and increasing wages. Wage increases in excess of productivity could easily be passed on to consumers in the form of price increases. The real income of many union members was fully or partially protected from inflation by the inclusion of cost-of-living adjustments in collective agreements, by which employees would receive wage increases linked to increases in the Consumer Price Index. Thus, the overall state of the product market offered little incentive for either employers or unions to question the industrial relations system (Block and McLennan 1985, pp. 337-82; Block 1990a, pp. 19-48).

Increasing Competition and Management Strategy

The unionized sector was disproportionately affected by widening competition in the late 1970s and early 1980s. This competition came primarily from two sources: worldwide competition in manufacturing and deregulation in transportation. For example, Block and McLennan (1985) point out that import penetration in highly unionized auto and basic steel sectors, which was negligible between the end of World War II and 1970, had increased 20 to 25 percent by 1980. In motor freight transportation, an industry in which deregulation commenced in 1976, the number of licenses issued increased by 1,000 in 1980, 4,000 in 1981, and 3,400 in 1983.[23] The airline industry was also affected by new entrants taking advantage of deregulation.[24]

Manufacturing and transportation also happened to be among the more heavily unionized sectors of the economy during this period. Whereas the overall percentage of employees represented by unions was 23.3 percent in 1983, the rates of union representation in manufacturing and transportation, respectively, were 30.5 percent and 46.2 percent.[25]

This competition, which was associated with declining market share and falling profits for the unionized firms, activated management. Many companies believed that the financial and product market competition facing them could no longer justify an industrial relations system characterized by ever-increasing wages and rigid rules that, while adopted to assure objective treatment of employees, often limited management's discretion to make production changes. In short, management believed that the rule-laden system of institutionalized adversarialism was costly and inefficient, and was often unwilling to continue to accept it.

These changes in the competitive environment, along with a legal system that permitted them wide latitude in making business decisions without negotiating with the union, spurred companies to reconsider their labor relations assumptions. Management began to use the flexibility in the legal system to make strategic choices about how they would administer their industrial relations (Block 1990a).

What drove the choices? The answer varied across situations. Sometimes it was a desire simply to control costs in the current production process to meet newly emerging competition. Sometimes it was a desire to act on long-dormant preferences to be nonunion by using tools that were not available before the late 1950s. Sometimes it was part of a broader product market strategy that required a reconfiguration of traditional labor relations (Block and McLennan 1985).

What were these management choices? They are depicted diagrammatically in figure 2.1. In the diagram, the traditional model of institutionalized adversarialism is depicted as a middle option. Management choices involved either maintaining a middle ground of institutionalized adversarialism, or moving toward extremes of cooperation or conflict. Some companies opted for deunionization, i.e., eliminating unions from their operations, to the extent possible.[26] Other companies moved toward cooperation with their unions, attempting to reduce the amount of adversarialism in the industrial relations system. Each of these two extreme options will be examined.[27]

Figure 2.1 Employer Labor Relations Strategies since the Late 1970s

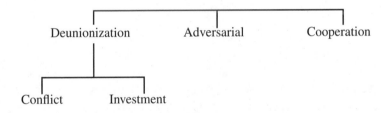

Deunionization.

Deunionization in the 1980s took two forms, deunionization through conflict and deunionization through investment. Companies that used the conflict form of deunionization would overtly try to rid themselves of unionism in existing facilities. The most common method was to make proposals during collective bargaining that the company knew were unacceptable to the union in order to force a strike. The company would then use its right to permanently replace striking workers with new employees. A decertification attempt would normally follow.[28] Even if the union did not strike and accepted the company's proposals, the employer would have reduced labor costs considerably and weakened the union's credibility. This strategy is consistent with the tactics of such companies as Phelps Dodge, Continental Airlines, and Greyhound Bus Lines, all of which hired permanent replacements during a strike.[29]

Deunionization through investment was done through unionized firms establishing new, nonunion facilities. In some cases, the firm would invest away from the union. Thus, the newer, more productive assets were invested in a nonunion facility. Eventually, the unionized facility becomes obsolete, resulting in reduced employment in the unionized sector of the firm. This occurred in the rubber tire industry. When industry capacity shifted from bias ply tires to radial tires in the late 1970s and early 1980s the industry made the choice to open new, nonunion plants outside of Akron. In the construction and trucking industries, many formerly unionized firms opened nonunion subsidiaries (Block and McLennan 1985; Walton, Cutcher-Gershenfeld, and McKersie 1994; Karper 1987; and Belzer 1994).

Cooperation

While some companies moved toward eliminating unionism in their organizations, other companies implemented the opposite strategy. While they were willing to accept unions, they rejected the rule-laden adversarialism associated with traditional bargaining. They advocated the creation of new, nonadversarial structures to facilitate communication and participation and joint decision making. They made a strategic decision to reduce costs by eliminating costs associated with adversarialism, thereby permitting the firm to exploit the knowledge of its workers and expand the knowledge base on which the firm could draw (Kochan, Katz, and McKersie 1994).

Such labor-management cooperation often broke down the barriers between mandatory and nonmandatory subjects of bargaining. Workers would be involved in product design, marketing, and other management prerogatives, often making changes in the production process. Financial information, which was only shared under the threat of legal action in adversarial bargaining, would be given to the union. Cooperation was based on notions of commonality of interest; if workers do not know the company's problems, they cannot help solve them. The presumption was that workers possess answers and solutions that they had been unwilling to share with management.

Many firms established joint committees on production processes and standards. Operating teams of workers, often self-managed, took control over the pace of work and how the work was done. These decisions were no longer the exclusive province of supervisors. Indeed, upper-level firm management often favored such systems because they reduced the need for supervisors.

Despite the seeming attractiveness of labor-management cooperation, there was still much reluctance to embrace the concept. Management, the legal representative of the shareholders, was often unwilling to be perceived as ceding its authority over the operation of the firm to the union. Thus, while much has been done at the workplace level to improve productivity, little has been done at the strategic level. Decisions such as what to produce, where to produce it, product design, and product pricing have been left in management's hands. Management has not been willing to give up its control over these major decisions.

Many unions also have been reluctant to embrace such a program. Their traditional role has been as an adversary to management—to protest management's actions where such protest was appropriate. Participating in cooperative programs could cause members to question the loyalty of their union representatives.[30]

In addition, the two extreme strategies of cooperation and deunionization are not mutually exclusive. The U.S. auto industry has been on the forefront of joint labor-management programs. At the same time, they continue to produce parts in Mexico.[31]

Determinants of Strategic Decisions

The common factor among all three choices—traditional adversarialism, deunionization, or cooperation—was that management made the decision. Management, with its control over capital investment decisions based on *First National Maintenance*, its interest in reducing employment costs, and its right to replace strikers if the situation came to that, generally had the greater bargaining power in the collective bargaining relationship. With minimal government intervention to offset that power, management's strategic interests generally dominated the unionized sector in the 1980s.[32]

What determined management's strategic decisions in industrial relations? There is no fixed answer; rather, there are multiple determinants. Clearly a key factor was management values. Management, as the property owner and initiator, decided the conceptual framework under which it viewed employment. Should the company's employees be viewed as a cost to be minimized or assets to be preserved because they create value? This question, laden with values, often underlay the labor relations strategy a company adopted. A view that employees primarily represent a cost to be minimized often resulted in conflict. On the other hand, a view that employees were assets to be preserved generally resulted in cooperation.

Another factor was how much strength the union had. In the auto industry, for example, it would be difficult for the company to pursue a complete policy of deunionization even if it were so inclined. The union is a substantial presence at General Motors, Ford, and Chrysler and would likely use its power where it has influence if they attempted to substantially deunionize. For example, in 1988, the United Auto Workers, by threatening local strikes and withdrawal from cooperative programs, forced Chrysler to change a decision to sell its parts subsidiary (Block 1990a).

The business strategy chosen by management often had an important impact on labor relations. A decision to be a low-cost, low-wage producer will normally encourage the employer to deunionize if sufficient concessions are not forthcoming. On the other hand, if more labor flexibility is required in a capital-intensive industry, the employer may prefer to work with the union. A high value-added strategy was pursued by Xerox. In this strategy, management needed the cooperation of the union representing its employees, and the two parties, Xerox and the Amalgamated Clothing and Textile Workers, took a cooperative approach (Block and McLennan 1985; Kochan, Katz, and McKersie 1994; Cutcher-Gershenfeld 1991).

The steel industry undertook a strategy of capacity reduction. As the problem in the industry was capacity and not cost, the steel industry basically maintained institutionalized adversarialism, with concessions (Block and McLennan 1985; Barnett and Schorsch 1984; Hoerr 1988).

Summary

During the period 1935-1977, the traditional system of institutionalized adversarialism dominated. It gave the union certain rights to negotiate over terms and conditions of employment. Because there was little competition for firms in the unionized industries, management strategy was generally passive or expansionary, neither of which was in conflict with the interest of unions in raising wages and protecting employees. As management's strategic decisions had little relationship to labor relations, there was little incentive to modify the adversarial system.

By the late 1970s, and certainly with the 1981 Supreme Court decision in *First National Maintenance*, management had acquired the right to make major strategic decisions without negotiating with the union. This coincided with increasing competitiveness in product markets. As some companies developed strategies associated with reductions in capacity or investment in new plant and equipment, their strategic decisions began to come into conflict with union interests. Thus, newly competitive product markets encouraged some managements to assert the dominance that law had given them in labor relations. This often involved challenging the long-established adversarial system of labor relations, either through deunionization or through cooperation. The result was a movement of industrial relations toward the extremes.

The Nonunion Employment Relations System

With declining unionization in the United States since the late 1950s, the major phenomenon in industrial relations that has occurred over the past thirty-five years is the rise of an actively nonunion sector. What are the means by which this occurred? Clearly, a major factor has been management ideology. Unlike management in Western Europe, which developed a rapprochement with unions in the first half of the twentieth century, management in the United States has never accepted the legitimacy of union representation for their employees.[33] While firms that were unionized during the period 1935-55 eventually learned to live with their unions through institutionalized adversarialism, firms that were not unionized during that period often determined to stay that way. They were aided in their task by the ambivalence that U.S. workers have long demonstrated toward unions and collective activity and the development of legal and management tools for union avoidance that evolved during the 1940s and 1950s (Perlman 1966; Sisson 1987).

Union avoidance was accomplished in two major ways, which may be described as the "soft" and "hard" systems. The soft system generally operated under the proposition that unionization could be avoided by making employees believe that unions were unnecessary. The hard methods operated under the proposition that unionization should be dealt with harshly, if it became an issue.

The Soft Approach

The soft method has been associated with such large firms as IBM, Delta Airlines (other than the unionized pilots), Federal Express, and Hewlett Packard. Such systems need not explicitly refer to unions or even mention unions as a concern. Rather, they are often developed under the assumption that it makes good business sense to treat employees fairly and equitably. These firms believe that such treatment, by its nature, reduces employee interest in unionization (Kochan, Katz, and McKersie 1994).

These soft systems developed personnel systems and practices that created consistency among employees, in essence emulating the systems of rules that resulted from collective bargaining. Increased authority was given to corporate personnel staffs to develop policies and to apply these policies fairly to all employees. Wages and benefit levels of these firms were generally competitive with unionized firms. In this way, management eliminated the major workplace abuses of the nonunion system while still maintaining authority.

Subfunctions that supported human resources began to develop. Recruitment and selection techniques developed to assure an appropriate match between the employee and organization. Firms invested in training and career development of employees to maximize their earnings potential. Pay systems were rationalized, linked to the external market, to the position, and to the employees' performance. Supporting performance appraisal systems were upgraded and rationalized. All of this reduced the amount of arbitrariness and supervisor favoritism in performance appraisal systems. Some firms developed formal grievance and complaint procedures for employees to use if they believed they were not treated fairly. Many firms developed participation plans, through which employees were involved in workplace decisions.

The soft approach operates not by reducing wages, per se, but by limiting the growth of overall labor costs through reducing the number of workers hired and providing management with flexibility to allocate labor in the manner that it wishes. It is based on the notion that the most important effect of unions in the firm is on the allocation of labor rather than on the wage rate. It tends to be most successful in firms in which labor costs represent a relatively small component of product costs, that are capital-intensive, that compete with unionized firms, and that are successful in their chosen product market. It is normally associated with deeply held values on the part of management to treat their employees well.

The Hard Approach

The second method, the hard approach, operates by using management authority and the tools and characteristics of the legal system to discourage employees from unionizing. The hard approach is designed to keep the union from becoming a topic of conversation among employees and, if necessary, to win a representation election if one was scheduled. Although more difficult to document through scientifically valid research, employers who choose his approach have used threats, harassment, and intimidation to discourage employees from supporting unionization. Although such behavior may be illegal, as discussed above, the penalties for such activity have generally not served as a deterrent. If an election is scheduled, employers have been able to use the election campaign and their control over information at the workplace to erode union support among employees.

Employee Participation Plans: A Soft or Hard Approach?

As can be seen, the soft approach tends to avoid legal issues in the hope that employees will not raise the matter of unionization. Legal strategies and use of the legal system are not important aspects of the soft approach. On the other hand, use of the legal system is an integral aspect of the hard approach.

Over the past fifteen years, however, legal questions have arisen under the soft approach when companies have instituted employee participation plans (EPPs). Although there is no legally accepted definition of an EPP, it may be defined as a structure or program under which firms solicit suggestions or input from employees on workplace issues. An EPP can be distinguished from traditional hierarchical decision making in a firm, under which management makes decisions based on only intramanagement consultation, with employees being informed of the decision and any effect on them.

An EPP can take on a range of structures. For example, one type of EPP involved monthly meetings among elected employees and management personnel in which company plans and programs would be communicated, problem areas identified, and suggestions for improvements solicited.[34] Another involved inviting employees, on a rotating basis, to monthly "rap sessions," during which company management would solicit questions and suggestions. Based on a management directive, representatives were elected along departmental lines by employees.[35]

Section 8(a)(2) of The National Labor Relations Act makes it an unfair labor practice for an employer "to dominate or interfere with the formation or administration of any labor organization or contribute financial or other support to it." A "labor organization," in turn, is defined very broadly in Section 2(5) as

> any organization of any kind, or agency, or employee representation committee or plan, in which employees participate and which exists for the purpose, in whole or in part, of dealing with employers concerning wages, rates of pay, hours of employment, or conditions of work.

These two sections together were designed to assure that employee representation was independent of the employer and that employees were protected in the right to choose whatever form of representation they wished; thus employees need not choose representation by a traditional union.

An important interpretation of Section 2(5) was issued in 1959, when the U.S. Supreme Court, in the *Cabot Carbon* case, ruled that the term "dealing with" in Section 2(5) was broader than the term "bargaining."[36] In *Cabot Carbon*, the employer had established employee committees consisting of elected employees serving one-year terms. The committees met monthly with plant management on working time and were designed to consider employees' ideas on matters of mutual interest to employees and management, and to handle employee grievances, although they could not issue a final decision. The monthly meetings addressed such issues as seniority, work schedules, and vacations, with the company often granting the committees' requests. Although the employer in *Cabot Carbon* did not enter into a collective bargaining agreement with the union, the Court ruled that the term "dealing with" encompassed activities in addition to bargaining. Thus, an employee structure could be found to be a labor organization even if the employer did not bargain with it.

Based on the broad definition of "dealing with" enunciated in *Cabot Carbon*, when employers began to establish EPPs, a fundamental question arose as to whether these structures, generally established and supported by the employer, were "labor organizations" under the NLRA and therefore illegally dominated, because the employer's relationship with that EPP was one of "dealing with" the EPP (Sockell 1984; U.S. Department of Labor 1986, 1987; Block and Cutcher-Gershenfeld 1992). Realizing that it was often important to obtain employee views on a variety of matters, nonunion employers viewed EPPs as a legitimate method of obtaining information from employees who otherwise had no desire to be unionized. Such employers did not necessarily view them as the type of organization the NLRA had attempted to outlaw in 1935.

Unions, on the other hand, viewed many such EPPs as creating an unlawful substitute labor organization that prevented employees from exercising their rights to select an independent bargaining agent. In that sense, many unions viewed these plans as precisely the type of structure that Congress had outlawed.

These different legal views mirrored the policy debate. Were EPPs a legal means by which management could work with employees in workplaces in which there was no desire to be unionized to improve productivity and quality, or were EPPs unlawful vehicles through which employers dominated employee representation structures to thwart the possibility of true, independent employee representation? Put differently, did EPPs enhance employee choice by giving employees a new option for representation, or did they impair employee choice by preventing them from exercising a choice for or against their own representative.

The 1992 NLRB and 1994 court decision in *Electromation*,[37] and the 1993 NLRB decision in *E.I. du Pont de Nemours*[38] have shed some light on the issue. In *Electromation*, the NLRB found that "action committees" created in January 1989 by a nonunion employer were unlawfully dominated labor organizations. The committees addressed five problem areas identified by the employer from meetings earlier that month involving randomly selected employees: absenteeism/infractions, no-smoking policy, communication network, pay progression, and attendance bonus. Each committee consisted of management personnel and six employees who had signed up. The committee members were asked to discuss their assigned problem areas with employees. Following a union recognition demand on February 13, 1989, the employer informed the committees that it could no longer participate in them, but that the committees could continue to meet on their own. After the attendance bonus committee submitted a proposal that was deemed unacceptable by the employer's controller, a second proposal submitted by that committee was acceptable to the controller but was never presented to the employer's president because of the union recognition campaign.[39]

The Board found, and the court agreed, that the Electromation action committees were illegal. First, the Court agreed with the Board that the involvement of the Electromation employees in the committees constituted "employee participation" within the meaning of Section 2(5). Second, the Board also found that the committees' roles constituted "dealing with" the employer, as they constituted a "bilateral mechanism" to present employee proposals to the employer.[40] Third, the subject matter of the "dealing" was terms and conditions of employment; e.g. pay, absenteeism/attendance, etc., as all of the matters that were assigned to the committees were employment related issues.[41]

On the other hand, the *Electromation* decisions suggest that EPPs that do not represent employees in terms and conditions of employment or deal with the employer on matters of terms and conditions of employment are legal. Thus, if the EPP dealt solely with production, efficiency, or quality issues (as compared to terms and conditions of employment), if it was independent, and if it did not represent employees, it would likely be legal.[42] The "bilateral mechanism" concept also implies that suggestion systems regarding terms or conditions of employment, in which an employer takes suggestions but makes the final decision without consulting with employees would also be legal.

That this might be the case was indicated in *du Pont*. Although *du Pont* involved a unionized firm, some of its lessons are instructive for nonunion employers as well. In *du Pont*, six safety committees and one fitness committee were found to be dominated labor organizations. The committees made proposals to management, to which management responded, and the committees had management personnel as full members. Thus, the "dealing with" criterion was met both inside and outside the committees. The employer established the committee's operating procedures, management committee members controlled the agenda and conducted the meetings, and the committees addressed matters involving terms and conditions of employment, some of which had been the subject of collective bargaining negotiations.[43]

In *du Pont*, the Board stated, however, that a brainstorming group to generate ideas was lawful because management could use or discard whatever ideas it wished.[44] A suggestion box system would not be unlawful because the suggestions come from individuals, not groups.[45] In neither case is there bilateral dealing. Similarly, a committee that focused solely on education programs or imparted information would not be unlawful, as the former does not involve terms or conditions of employment,[46] and the latter is not bilateral.[47]

Overall, then, these two key cases suggest that a nonunion employer may establish an EPP that is designed to address solely production, efficiency, and quality issues. For these issues, the interactions between the employees involved in the EPP and management may take any form desired, e.g., suggestions, consultation, or proposals. On the other hand, to the extent such an EPP addresses issues involving terms or conditions of employment (such as wages, vacations, or production bonuses), it will be found unlawful if it is established as an employee representative and if the employer does more than take suggestions or ideas.

Development of Legislation and Law on Individual Employment Rights

While the period since the mid-1950s was a difficult one for employees exercising collective bargaining rights in the workplace, it saw an expansion of legislation affecting individual employees. Clearly, the most important federal and state laws have been those prohibiting employment discrimination on the basis of race, gender, origin, age, and disability. Privacy rights have been addressed through legislation limiting polygraph testing. Some state courts have placed limits on the extent to which employers can terminate employees, essentially calling into question the long-standing principle of employment-at-will (an employee may be discharged for good cause, bad cause, or no cause at all so long as no other laws are violated). Other states have found some rights for employees to have their private social lives free from employer intervention. Recently the Family and Medical Leave Act of 1993 has required employers to provide pregnant employees with up to twelve weeks of unpaid leave, with a right to return to the job. Workplace safety and health has been addressed through the Occupational Safety and Health Act.[48]

These laws are far too broad and complex to attempt a summary of them here. What is important however, for our purposes, is the method by which these law are enforced. Unlike the NLRA, which is enforced in a uniform manner by one agency, the laws are enforced by the courts. Litigation can be arduous and expensive, and damage awards can be substantial. Such a system makes access burdensome for employees, who generally do not have the resources of employers. In addition, if the employer does not prevail, the damage awards can be very high.

Employers also complain about the burden from the regulations associated with these laws. Equal employment opportunity laws, for example, generally involve keeping detailed records of employees, applicants, and their placement within organizations. Accommodation is often required. Smaller employers, especially, claim that it is extremely costly to them to maintain the records and to comply with the law. While employers seem to accept the principle behind laws protecting individual employees, they seem to believe that the methods of administering the laws are extremely burdensome to them.[49]

What is most significant, however, about these laws, is that while they are complex, they impose substantial record-keeping burdens on employers, and they may require some accommodation of individual employees, they are in no sense a broad-based regulation of employment. Rather, they operate at the extremes, addressing only those situations in which employment decisions come into conflict with social norms.

The antidiscrimination laws, which are clearly the most important of this legislation, are targeted at eliminating *differential treatment* between majority employees and employees in protected classes, consistent with individualistic values in the United States—people should be rewarded economically on the basis of market forces, not on the basis of personal characteristics unrelated to the market. So long as employers do not treat employees differentially based on race, gender, religion, disability status, or other such protected status, employers may do what they wish under these laws. Thus, as an example, it would be unlawful for an employer to provide health insurance for male employees and not for female employees. It would not, however, be unlawful for an employer to provide no health insurance at all.

Thus, in general, these laws do not regulate the terms and conditions of employment and day-to-day treatment of employees on the job.[50] This is still left to the individual bargain or the collectively negotiated agreement between the employer and the employees.

Summary and Concluding Observations

Based on the discussion in this chapter, it is clear that the letter of National Labor Relations Act makes employee choice the major value to be protected. The law is designed to protect the right of employees to make a choice regarding union representation. If the employees choose representation, the employer has the obligation to negotiate with the employees' chosen representative.

The last sixty years, however, have seen a continual, piecemeal expansion of employer rights in the industrial relations system. In union organizing campaigns, employers generally have daily and almost unlimited access to employees to present their views on unionization. Unions are generally prevented from entering the workplace, and employee solicitation is limited to lunch periods and break times.

In collective bargaining, the overall direction of the law has been to permit the parties to bargain with minimal government involvement, and to engage in self-help as they see fit. Thus, the law permits employers to exclude from bargaining most decisions that are based on capital investment. In addition, the law permits a bargaining strategy in which both sides can make proposals they know to be unacceptable, and attempt to force it on the other party. The nature of the employment relationship, however, limits the extent to which the union can benefit from such a strategy. If the employer suffers economic harm and loses business, the result is normally lost employment and lost jobs.

On the other hand, the law permits the employer to make an unacceptable proposal and stick to it, forcing the union to strike or to accept the proposal. If the union strikes, the employer has the option of replacing the workers, eventually eliminating the collective bargaining relationship. In essence, the evolution of the law of bargaining has resulted in the anomalous situation in which an employer, exercising rights to bargain under the NLRA, can actually destroy the collective bargaining relationship.

This evolution has been the result of the case-by-case approach to legal decision making under the NLRA. There is no mechanism under the Act for considering the effect of any decision on any other legal doctrine.[51] Thus, while each of these decisions may be justifiable on its own, when they are taken together, they give the employer who is inclined to use the legal system and resist employee choice a powerful set of tools to accomplish its aims.

Overall, the industrial relations legal system gives employers a great deal of discretion over how they wish to practice industrial relations. Some employers, operating within the industrial relations/collective bargaining system in the United States, choose to recognize the legitimacy of employees' choice of a union to represent them and to cooperate with that union. Such firms, in honoring this employee choice of representative, often involve their employees in various aspects of the business, including production, and keep employees informed of the company's financial position. The union is the conduit through which the company interacts with its employees.

Similarly, many nonunion employers also deal with their employees fairly, openly, and honestly, often developing systems by which employees can participate in making decisions related to quality and production. Although these systems tend to work through the company's production organization rather than through the union, the result is often similar to labor-management cooperation in unionized systems.[52] Generally, such firms operate to make unionization unnecessary to employees. Employee choice for unionization is rarely an issue in these companies.[53]

Other employers, however, operate differently. These employers use all aspects of the law to the extreme. They may even step over the line between legal and illegal activity, knowing that the penalties are minimal for such activity. Such employer activity, even if legal, may have the effect of impairing the mechanism by which employees may choose whether to be represented by a union.

The next two chapters will provide examples of both kinds of employers. Relying on the testimony from the Dunlop commission hearings, chapter 3 will present examples of cooperative labor-management relations in both unionized and nonunion firms, the former honoring the employees' choice to unionize, and the latter making the choice of unionism a nonissue. Chapter 4 will present examples of an underside of labor-management relations, where employers overtly prevent their employees from exercising their right of choice.

NOTES

1. All references to the text of the National Labor Relations Act as amended as based on Oberer, Hanslowe, and Heinsz (1994, pp. 41-81).

2. See, for example, *Pacific Intermountain Express, Inc.*, 105 N.L.R.B. 480 (1953).

3. Millis and Brown (1950, ch. 5). Interestingly, Canada, which has developed provincial labor law systems patterned on the Wagner Act model, has not adopted the election as the primary means of determining employee support for a union. Canadian provincial boards use varying types of membership evidence. In addition to elections, valid membership evidence in Canada includes employee payment of dues to a labor organization and signed union membership cards. See Adams (1994, pp. 7-55 to 7-80).

4. See, for example, "Testimony Heard on Extension of Taft Act to Nonprofit Hospitals," *BNA Daily Labor Report,* No. 71, 1973 (4/12/73), pp. A-8 to A-9; "Extension of Taft-Hartley Act to Nonprofit Hospitals Predicted,: *BNA Daily Labor Report*, No. 27, 1974 (2/7/74), pp. A-3 to A-4; and "House Passes Measure Putting Nonprofit Hospitals under NLRA," *BNA Daily Labor Report*, No. 105, 1974)5/31/74), pp. A-15 to A-17.

5. *NLRB* v. *Jones and Laughlin Steel Corporation*, 301 U.S. 1 (1937).

6. Legal protection did not extend to all union activities that to this point had been used successfully during the union organizing drives of the 1930s. In *NLRB* v. *Fansteel*, 306 U.S. 240 (1939), the U.S. Supreme Court ruled that an employer did not commit an unfair labor practice when it discharged employees who engaged in a sit-down strike in which employees occupied the employer's premises. The Court found that the unfair labor practices committed by Fansteel did not give the union license to act unlawfully by seizing the employer's property. In later years, the NLRA protection was removed (thereby permitting employer discharge or discipline) from other union activity designed to pressure employers. For example, Supreme Court decisions removed NLRA protection from employee acts of disloyalty during a strike (*NLRB* v. *Local 1229, International Brotherhood of Electrical Workers*, 346 U.S. 464, 1953) and a union slowdown while negotiations were ongoing (*NLRB* v. *Insurance Agents International Union*, 361 U.S. 477, 1960).

7. 324 U.S. 792.

8. *NLRB* v. *Virginia Electric and Power Co.* 314 U.S. 469 (1941); Millis and Brown (1950, pp. 174-189); Block, Wolkinson, and Kuhn (1988, pp. 220-240).

9. Block, Wolkinson, and Kuhn (1988); *American Tube Bending Co.*, 44 N.L.R.B. 121 (1942), enf. den. other grounds, 134 F.2d 993 (2nd Cir., 1943); *Clark Bros.*, 70 N.L.R.B. 802 (1946), enf'd 163 F.2d 373 (end Cir., 1947); *Bonwit Teller*, 96 N.L.R.B. 608 (1951), enf'd 197 F.2d 640

(2nd Cir., 1952); and *Livingston Shirt Co.*, 107 N.L.R.B. 400 (1954). An employer may not deliver a captive audience speech within twenty-four hours of the election. See *Peerless Plywood, Inc.* 107 N.L.R.B. 427 (1954).

10. See cases cited in Block, Wolkinson, and Kuhn (1988).

11. *NLRB* v. *Babcock and Wilcox Co.*, 351 U.S. 105 (1956).

12. Block and Wolkinson (1986); Block, Wolkinson, and Kuhn (1988); Avery (1989); *Lechmere, Inc.* v. *NLRB*, 112 S.Ct. 841 (1992).

13. In the early 1940s, approximately 80 percent of all elections resulted in an employee choice for representation (a union victory). Since that time, the percentage of elections in which employees have chosen representation has consistently declined to approximately 48 percent. See Block and Wolkinson (1986) and NLRB A*nnual Report*s, various years.

14. See Section 8(d) of the National Labor Relations Act.

15. *NLRB* v. *Insurance Agents International Union*, 371 U.S. 477 (1960) as reported in Oberer et al. (1986, pp. 493-494).

16. Interestingly, Section 1 of the NLRA states that the inequality of bargaining power between employees who do not have freedom of association or complete liberty of contract and employers organized in the corporate form was one of the bases for the passage of the Wagner Act.

17. *NLRB* v. *Wooster Division of Borg-Warner Corp.*, 356 U.S. 342 (1958). The parties may not negotiate over illegal terms and conditions of employment, such as those that discriminate against females and minorities. Canadian (provincial) labour law does not draw a distinction between mandatory and permissive subjects—all subjects are negotiable. See Adams (1994, pp. 10-96).

18. *Fibreboard Products Corp.* v. *NLRB* 379 U.S. 203 (1964); *Ozark Trailers, Inc.*, 161 N.L.R.B. 561 (1966); *UAW* v. *NLRB*, 470 F.2d 422 (D.C. Cir., 1972); *First National Maintenance Corp.* v. *NLRB*, 452 U.S. 666 (1981); *Otis Elevator Co.*, 269 N.L.R.B. 861 (1984); *Dubuque Packing Co.*, 303 N.L.R.B. No. 66 (1991), enf. 143 LRRM 3001 (D.C. Cir., 1993). Regardless of whether the employer must bargain with the union over the decision, the employer must always bargain with the union over the effects of such a decision.

19. Cooke (1983, pp. 402-414). Such unit challenges generally involve both legal and strategic considerations. Generally, the union is attempting to structure a unit that contains a majority of employees whom it believes will vote for union representation, while the employer is attempting to structure a unit it believes will contain a majority of employees that will vote against representation.

20. See, for example, Weiler (1983, pp. 1769-1827); Freeman and Medoff (1984, ch. 15); Kleiner (1984, pp. 234-243).

21. *H.K. Porter Co.* v. *NLRB*, 397 U.S. 99)1970); Prosten (1978); Cooke (1985, pp. 163-178).

22. Although the Canadian labor boards do not dictate the terms of agreements, they scrutinize and observe negotiations to a much greater extent than the NLRB, and possess authority to intervene in negotiations. The NLRB has no such authority. See, for example, Block (1994).

23. See Block and McLennan (1985) and Belzer (1994).

24. See Block and McLennan (1985) and Capelli (1987). Voos (1994) contends that the increased competition so affecting unions was not inevitable; that it resulted from a series of policy choices designed to encourage greater product market competition in the U.S. economy.

25. See BNA *Daily Labor Report*, No. 31, 1985 (2/14/85), pp. B-1 to B-5.

26. Hirsch (1991) found that during the 1970s and early 1980s, nonunion firms substantially outperformed their unionized counterparts in terms of such indicators as profits and rate of return. To the extent that this was known, or even sensed, by the management of unionized firms, the incentive to deunionize was enhanced. See also Kleiner et al. (1987).

27. These three options are somewhat consistent with the strategies that have been designated escape, forcing, and fostering. See Walton, Cutcher-Gershenfeld, and McKersie (1994).

28. Consistent with the principle of employee choice, the NLRB has established a procedure by which employees may decertify a union, e.g., choose to vote out a union that has representation rights. The term "decertify" is based on the "certification" of the union by the Board that follows a vote by employees in favor of representation.

29. These strikes were heavily covered in the business press. For coverage of the Phelps Dodge Strike, see for example, Kathleen A. Hughes, "Phelps Dodge Is Determined to Continue Operations at Copper Mines Despite Strike," *Wall Street Journal,* July 5, 1983, p. 8; National Guard Troops Sent to Morenci, Ariz., In Phelps Dodge Strike," *Wall Street Journal,* August 19, 1983, p. 24; "Phelps Dodge Corp. Reopens Copper Unit But Strike Continues," *Wall Street Journal,* August 22, 1983, p. 36; "Phelps Dodge Is Sued by United Steelworkers Over Current Strike,: *Wall Street Journal,* September 12, 1983, p. 24: "Phelps Dodge May Have Tamed its Unions," *Business Week,* September 26, 1983, p. 39; "Phelps Dodge Strikers Lose Round in Ruling by NLRB on Union," W*all Street Journal,* September 13, 1984, p. 49; "Phelps Dodge to Close Copper Smelting Plant In Arizona Temporarily," *Wall Street Journal,* December 26, 1984, p. 18. See also, Fillippelli (1990, pp. 409-411). For coverage of the Continental Airlines Strike, see for example, "Continental Airlines Says Strike Would Cause Service Suspensions," *Wall Street Journal,* August 12, 1983, p. 4; "Continental Airlines to Fire Employees Who Stay on Strike," *Wall Street Journal,* August 15, 1983, p. 6; "Continental Airlines Says It is Hiring Workers to Replace Strikers," *Wall Street Journal,* August16, 1983, p. 8; Robert S. Greenberger, "Striking Back: More Firms Get Tough And Keep Operating In Spite of Walkouts," *Wall Street Journal,* October 11, 1983, p. 1; "Continental Air, Pilots Suspend Negotiations," *Wall Street Journal,* December 22, 1983, p. 30. For coverage of the Greyhound Strike, see for example, "Greyhound Lines Inc. Union's Bargainers Agree To Call a Strike Thursday," *Wall Street Journal,* February 23, 1990, p. A4; Robert Tomshio, "Greyhound Ends New Talks Abruptly, Accuses Union of Continuing Violence," *Wall Street Journal,* March 19, 1990, p. A20; Robert Tomshio, "Union Offers End to Strike at Greyhound," *Wall Street Journal,* May 23, 1990, p. A9; "Greyhound Union to Stop Payment of Strike Benefits," *Wall Street Journal,* September 5, 1990, p. B6.

30. For an excellent study of the conflicts labor-management cooperation poses for union leaders, see Kochan, Katz, and Mower (1984).

31. For discussions of collective bargaining in the U.S. auto industry, see, for example, Block and McLennan (1985); Katz (1985); Katz and McDuffie (1994).

32. See Kochan, Katz, and McKersie (1994); and Block (1990a).

33. See, for example, Adams (1981, pp. 277-293); and Sisson (1987). The conventional wisdom among researchers is that Canadian employers are also more accepting of unions and collective bargaining than their U.S. counterparts. See, for example, Meltz (1990, pp. 46-52).

34. *NLRB* v. *Scott and Fetzer Co.,* 111 LRRM 2673 (C.A. 6, 1982).

35. *Airstream, Inc.* v. *NLRB,* 131 LRRM 2899 (C.A. 6, 1989).

36. *NLRB* v. *Cabot Carbon Co.,* 44 LRRM 2204.

37. 309 N.L.R.B. No. 163 (1992), enf. 147 LRRM 2257 (C.A. 6, 1994).

38. 311 N.L.R.B. No. 88 (1993).

39. See Block (1993).

40. 147 LRRM at 2267.

41. 147 LRRM at 2265-67.

42. 147 LRRM at 2264.

43. 311 N.L.R.B. No. 88, p. 4.

44. 311 N.L.R.B. No. 88 at p. 2. But the Board also found that, where a union represented the employees, such a brainstorming group could not discuss matters that could be addressed in negotiations (311 N.L.R.B. at p. 4).

45. 311 N.L.R.B. No. 88, p. 2.

46. 311 N.L.R.B. No. 8, p. 3.

47 In *du Pont*, the employer was also found to have violated the law by responding positively to a safety committee proposal for a new welding shop and a fitness committee proposal for development of a recreational area because the employer had previously rejected similar proposals from the union.

48. An excellent summary of these laws can be found in U.S. Department of Labor and U.S. Department of Commerce (1994, pp. 129-133).

49. It has been asserted that these laws have reduced the need for collective representation and employee interest in unions because they provide governmental protection from employer abuses. See, for example, Nash (1985, pp. 600-604). The empirical evidence for this propostion is mixed. Compare Neumann and Rissman (1984) (evidence in support of the proposition) with Block, Mahoney, and Corbitt (1987) (evidence against the proposition).

50. Exceptions to this statement are the following: the Employee Retirement and Income Security Act, which establishes uniform standards for pension plans; the Fair Labor Standards Act, which establishes minimum wage and overtime (for covered employees) requirements; the Family Medical Leave Act, which provides for up to twelve weeks of unpaid leave for the birth of a child; and the Worker Adjustment and Retraining Notification Act (WARN), which requires covered employers to provide employees with sixty days notice of a plant closing or large layoff.

51. See, for example, Block (1990b).

52. One major difference between labor-management cooperation in unionized and nonunion firms is that in the latter, the company may unilaterally decide to withdraw from cooperation at any time, while there is no mechanism for employee withdrawal. In other words, the system is unilaterally determined. In unionized firms, on the other hand, the system is negotiated between the employer and the legal representatives of the employees.

53. It is, of course, true that some employees in these companies are interested in unionization. (See for example, *Texas Instruments, Inc.* v. *NLRB*, 627 F.2d 822 (C.A. 6, 1981) and *IBM Corp.*, 265 N.L.R.B. 638 (1982). However, there does not appear to be a great deal of broad-based employee support for union representation in these companies.

CHAPTER 3

Labor-Management Cooperation in the United States

The decentralization of industrial relations in the United States has resulted in numerous examples of innovation in collective bargaining and some examples of nontraditional employee relations in nonunion firms. This chapter will discuss some of those programs, as they were presented at the Dunlop Commission hearings.

For unionized firms, these programs will be discussed in the context of two themes that emerged from the hearings: the role of government, and the avoidance of legalism. Following the discussion of the unionized sector, innovations in the nonunion sector will be discussed.

The Role of Government

One of the key subthemes coming out of the historical analysis in the previous chapter is the role of government. At least since Taft-Hartley was enacted, the role of government in labor relations has been seen as comparable to that of a judge, to be called upon only when needed. Another way to view government's role is that of an umpire who sees that bargaining takes place within acceptable limits.[1] The two governmental labor relations institutions reflect this view. The National Labor Relations Board (NLRB) only addresses charges brought to it; in essence, it is an adjudicatory agency. The Federal Mediation and Conciliation Service (FMCS) was created to help resolve disputes only when called upon by the parties. During the term of the contract, it provides lists of arbitrators to rule on grievances if requested by the parties. Many states have similar structures. Thus, the major governmental institutions were designed to be reactive.

In contrast, an examination of labor-management innovation often shows a more activist governmental role. Two models seem especially salient. One is the facilitation by local and county government institutions in the Louisville, Kentucky area. A second model, more traditional than the Louisville model, can be found in the activities of the FMCS in encouraging parties to work together.

The Louisville Model

For years, Louisville had a reputation for labor-management conflict; indeed, in the 1970s it was often referred to as Strike City, USA.[2] The mayor of Louisville estimated that poor labor-management relations cost the community 35,000 to 40,000 jobs in 1980-81. In the early 1980s, the Mayor's office began convening a group from the labor community, the local Chamber of Commerce, and government to offer solutions to labor-management problems in the community. With support from Ford, Philip Morris (both large local employers) and other companies, a Labor-Management Center was established at the University of Louisville.

The result of all this was an infrastructure of labor-management government unity that created an environment for cooperation. Much of this was manifested in training structures. The Kentuckiana Education and Workforce Development Initiative (KEWDI) focused on workforce development. Governed cooperatively by a collaborative arrangement among business, education, labor, and government, KEWDI conducts an annual survey of 1600 businesses in the Louisville area on the skill needs of employers. KEWDI has fourteen industry groupings, thus providing sufficient specialization for its constituency. It creates and maintains a training data base through a consortium of seventeen postsecondary educational institutions in the metropolitan area.

Louisville area officials, however, believed that in addition to accomplishing training and skill identification objectives, the training-based collaboration has had spillover effects into labor relations. This can be seen through two relationships.

Philip Morris, Inc. and Bakery, Confectionery, and Tobacco Workers Union, Local 16T.[3] Philip Morris has 2700 employees in the Louisville area, with 1700 of those employees represented by Local 16T. Prior to 1978, the parties were in a classic adversarial relationship. Each negotiation was preceded by a strike threat, with the union finally making good on its continual threats in 1977, when the parties experienced a six week strike. The adversarial system of bargaining, as it had developed at Philip Morris, was extremely stressful and costly to the parties. In anticipation of a strike that seldom came, the company would build up its inventories with a great deal of overtime, which was followed by shortened workweeks. This resulted in greater costs for the company, both in terms of overtime preceding the end of the contract and, no doubt, in experience ratings for unemployment insurance after the strike due to the layoffs.

The union also realized the hardship this placed on the members, who would be required to work long hours before the strike deadline—a tiring schedule that reduced leisure time considerably. A spell of unemployment would then result, either because of a strike or because layoffs would occur while the company pared down the inventory built up in anticipation of the strike.

After the 1977 strike, the parties decided to change. They developed a Long-Term Agreement (LTA), which was signed in 1979. The first LTA had a duration of nine years. The terms of the agreement would be renegotiated every three years, but there would be binding arbitration if there was no agreement as a result of the interim negotiations. In 1986, the parties extended the LTA for six years, to 1994. In 1992 negotiations, it was extended until 1997.

Among the most important accomplishments for the union was a provision for transfer rights to a new company facility in Carrabus County, North Carolina, and guaranteed income protection for those employees who did not transfer. Significantly for the union, Philip Morris did not oppose unionization in the new facility. The company had been able to operate successfully while unionized, and it did not wish to alienate other unions in other plants. Interestingly, Philip Morris was the object of much criticism from other firms in the Carrabus County area for paying high wages and accepting unions.

What were the results of the LTA? Grievance activity has been down by 90 percent since 1979. In 1988, the parties relaxed work rules, reduced the number of job classifications from 90 to 11, and negotiated a no-layoff guarantee except in the event of a decline in volume below a preset amount of production. In other words, if market share was maintained, there would be no layoffs. The parties also developed an employee development and training program with company-paid tuition and fees. The training would be both general college and vocational education and training specific to the needs of Philip Morris. The parties also agreed to joint labor-management safety committees and a managed health care plan. The latter met the company's interest in cost savings and the union's interest in coverage.

The company credited the efforts of the Mayor of Louisville in bringing labor and management together as a key factor in the improved relationship at Philip Morris. The Mayor's efforts, in the view of the company, created a new openness. Involvement in community and civic projects provided a vehicle for labor and management to work together on issues of common interest outside of the plant. They became acquainted with each other, and the good will carried over.

Louisville Gas and Electric and IBEW Local 2100.[4] The union at Louisville Gas and Electric was initially certified in 1980. The first two negotiations were settled only after strikes. The next two contracts were settled without strikes, but they were difficult negotiations—the first 1989 collective agreement was rejected by a 2-1 vote.

Following the 1989 negotiations, the parties agreed to change the relationship. They put forty labor and management officials plus the state and federal mediators that had been working with them through joint labor-management training in 1992. They also changed the bargaining process from traditional positional bargaining to mutual gains bargaining. The latter bases negotiations on an understanding of interests rather than a hardening of bargaining positions. In mutual gains bargaining, the parties used side-by-side problem solving and bargained without notes.[5] This clarified the issues being discussed, and it was successful. The parties came to an agreement without a mediator. They have since initiated mutual gains procedures in the grievance process.

Consistent with the Louisville culture, Louisville Gas and Electric and Local 2100 have been part of a community infrastructure to help others. They have assisted the Louisville Symphony Orchestra and the American Federation of Musicians in establishing mutual gains bargaining. They have also had some contacts with the management of the Louisville Zoo and the union representing zoo employees. Just as the facilitative community in Louisville helps the parties, the parties are giving back to the community through their aid to civic institutions.

The FMCS Assertive Availability Model

A second model may be called the "assertive availability" model. Such a model is more activist than the traditional FMCS model. The traditional FMCS role was to become involved, if asked, at the point at which the parties were on strike or close to a strike. It was designed to end labor conflict already initiated, or to avoid imminent labor conflict. Under the assertive availability model, FMCS would intervene, if asked to encourage the parties to move towards a cooperative relationship, thus preventing conflict before it starts.

The activities of the FMCS have traditionally been reactive but supportive. Over the last decade, however, the FMCS has expanded the activities of its mediators. In addition to the traditional role of the FMCS in resolving contract disputes and providing lists of arbitrators, FMCS mediators have increasingly become involved in helping parties use more interest-based bargaining approaches and move towards improved labor-management relations during the life of an agreement. FMCS has also aided joint labor-management groups (community or workplace-based) through a competitive federal grant program that provides modest funding for initiation or extension of innovative joint programs.

As an example of the expanded role of FMCS, management and the union at the Reynolds Aluminum plant in Sheffield, Alabama used FMCS to provide training on Relationships by Objectives, which in turn helped to facilitate their relationship. The efforts of Lyondell and the OCAW and Healthspan Corporation in Minneapolis were also supported by FMCS.

Reynolds Metals, Sheffield, Alabama and International Association of Machinists.[6] This aluminum casting facility employs 2200 people. The IAM is one of fourteen different unions in the facility—twelve craft unions, one production unit, and one guard unit. The plant was opened in 1941, and for the first forty years of existence was characterized by an adversarial relationship. Around 1980, the parties developed CHAMPS—Cooperative Hourly Management Problem-Solving Teams—to discuss work situations. In 1985, the parties used the FMCS to provide them with additional training, and they began to work together for job preservation and job satisfaction. They developed quality teams in all departments. All fourteen unions have agreed to worker participation and plant gainsharing; thus everybody works to improve the financial condition of the business and shares in those gains. They have recently built a world-class casting operation at Sheffield and this was largely a result of their good relationship. The unions provided their support by making job classification changes; where there were previously fourteen classifications, there is now only one. Return on investment at the new casting operation is 18 to 21 percent, exceeding expectations.

Lyondell Petrochemical Co. and the Oil, Chemical and Atomic Workers Union.[7] The company began operations in 1919 as Sinclair. It was merged into Atlantic Richfield in 1968, and it became the Lyondell Division of Atlantic Richfield in 1985. In 1993, it entered into a limited partnership with Citgo and its parent, the national petroleum company of Venezuela. The company has 720 hourly employees represented by the Oil, Chemical and Atomic Workers (OCAW). It had a very adversarial history under Sinclair and Atlanta Richfield. Under Lyondell, the management philosophy changed to one of employee involvement and partnership. The company made a decision to involve OCAW. The services of FMCS were enlisted to teach the leadership of the union and the refinery management about win-win bargaining. A joint steering committee was established to continue cooperative efforts without circumventing the collective agreement. Workers and management were sent to other unionized sites where cooperative efforts were in place, and FMCS conducted committee effectiveness training. The parties continue to work on developing a mutually agreeable partnership.

Lyondell wants a limited partnership, in which management has the responsibility, liability, accountability for running the business. The union tends to be uncomfortable with a the notion of a limited partnership, and wants to deal with management as an equal. Although the parties are continuing to feel their way through their relationship, they have many years of adversarialism to overcome.

Healthspan Corporation (Minneapolis) and Service Employees International Union Local 113.[8] Healthspan is a not-for-profit health care system headquartered in Minneapolis. It has 15,000 employees in Minnesota, and provides health care for 27 percent of the market in the Twin Cities. Service Employees International Union (SEIU) Local 113 represents 2000 employees with Healthspan. Other unions representing Healthspan employees are the Minnesota Nurses Association, Local 70 of the Operating Engineers International Union, Minnesota Licensed Practical Nurses Association, the Association of Diagnostic Technicians, and UA (Plumbers and Pipefitters) Local 561.

The parties' innovative relationship began in 1983, when representatives from Local 113 and the other labor organizations began meeting with representatives from United and Children's Hospitals in St. Paul to explore options and expand the hospital-labor organization relationships. In 1984, because several hospitals bargained as a group, a multi-hospital labor-management committee structure was developed. Initial assistance in the form of training was provided by the FMCS. Management and labor selected their own committee representatives and determined length of terms.

In 1985, United and Childrens' and the unions received an FMCS cooperation grant of $50,000 to develop a committee structure and to initiate joint projects on absenteeism, cost control, nursing scheduling, career opportunity programs, and cross-training for nursing staff. The FMCS-required 10 percent match was split between the hospitals and the unions. After the grant ended, the parties continued joint funding and supervision of a paid coordinator.

In April 1988, United's parent, Health One, merged with Health Central. The labor-management processes expanded in the new company. The parties, however, were at a turning point when a management-initiated Continuous Quality Improvement (CQI) plan was held up by the unions to secure labor participation in the design and leadership. Eventually, with help from a private organization, the National Center for Dispute Settlement, a new committee was created, the Health One Labor/Management CQI Council. The parties agreed that they would be equal partners, and they developed a written cooperative partnership agreement.

In March 1993, Health One and Lifespan merged to form Healthspan. Lifespan, although organized, had maintained a more traditional relationship. After the merger, new labor-management processes needed to be developed. FMCS and the Minnesota Bureau of Mediation Services provided funding and assistance towards the establishment of a Metropolitan Hospitals Labor/Management Council, composed of twenty hospitals, nine unions, and a separate Twin Cities Area Labor/Management Council, which was co-chaired by a human resources officer from Healthspan and a local official from SEIU. As a result of the efforts of the Labor/Management Council, the Council of Hospital Corporations (CHC), which is the hospital trade association, has examined existing labor relations practices and has developed goals supportive of the mutual gains-equal partners approach. Local 113 and CHC negotiated a contract using a mutual gains bargaining approach. They also concluded successful mutual gains bargaining. Both the CHC and Healthspan agreements establish a joint approach to work redesign and state that no layoffs will occur as a result of work redesign.

The Healthspan co-sponsorship agreement includes the corporation's employee relations principles, an outline of its labor-management partnership structures, a code of trust to guide dealings, the relationship to the collective bargaining agreement, management policy, and the parties' views on employment security. It was approved by the Labor/Management CQI Council. The cosponsorship agreement does not modify the collective bargaining agreement.

What are the key features of the Healthspan-SEIU system? Any item on which both parties can agree may be discussed in the partnership. A corporate document that covers all subsidiaries requires decentralized decision making at sites. Management believes its union members supported CQI, while labor feels that management is interested in the security and well-being of employees. There are to be no layoffs due to CQI. The arrangement is voluntary and is reevaluated yearly. Neither side will withdraw without first seeking the intervention of a third party who will attempt to resolve the problems leading to the proposed withdrawal.

The support structure for the partnership includes a Joint Labor Management Council (JLMC), operating unit (hospital) LMCs and bargaining unit LMCs. The JLMC has twenty-five members, including executive management and union leadership, with labor and management co-chairs. The operating unit councils are approved by the corporate council. There are thirteen bargaining unit councils, which meet once per month and are co-chaired by labor and management. They have established budgets, ground rules, and meeting agendas developed by the co-chairs. Each organization also has ad hoc CQI teams that are project-based.

What has been done? The CQI team solved problems with linen distribution in one hospital by instituting a just-in-time delivery system that saved $3 million dollars in inventory costs. There is a joint effort to reduce costs by $10 to $17 million at Unity and Mercy Hospitals. Working with a physician steering committee, a CQI team is jointly restructuring service delivery, with the LMC as the link between the redesigned processes and the workforce. A July 1991 closure of a downtown Minneapolis hospital that was losing millions of dollars per year tested the effectiveness of the joint effort. Facing projected unemployment insurance and severance payments estimated to be from $10 to $18 million, the joint committee was able to design a process of closure costing only $500,000, with 90 percent of the 1,475 employees placed in new jobs.

Summary

As can be seen, government has played two different kinds of roles. One, based on the Louisville model, may be called "direct encouragement." By bringing the parties together and encouraging them to set aside differences, structures are created. By the government taking the position that labor-management cooperation is the preferred method of dealing with workplace problems, government has legitimized such relationships. Given the current legal structure, this is perhaps the most a government is able to do to encourage cooperation.

A second model may be called the "assertive availability" model. In this model, government stands ready with resources to help parties, but offers these assertively before being asked. The activities of the FMCS in the Reynolds-IAM, Lyondell-OCAW, and Healthspan examples, and the Minnesota Bureau of Mediation Services in the Healthspan examples demonstrate government supporting cooperative efforts with both human and financial resources. This is the traditional role of government in the United States. It is supportive, but still noninterventionist.

Avoidance of Legalism

The law is associated with an adversarial process. The assertion of legal rights by one party vis-a-vis another party is, by definition, adversarial. Thus, it is not surprising that a key characteristic of innovative relationships is the absence of legalism. Innovative workplace relations do not rely on legal rights; rather they move beyond them. The law, as it has evolved, gives the employer the right to overtly resist unionism during the organizing campaign. Even if the union is certified, the law has given the employer the right to use the legal system to continue opposition to unionism and to contain unions. In other words, the employer has the legal right to continue to oppose unionism in its facilities whether the union is certified or not. Despite this, in the examples to be discussed in this section, there is little reliance of the employer on these legal rights. Ford Motor Company has been one of the most innovative companies vis-a-vis its relationship with the union representing its employees (the United Auto Workers). Peter Pestillo, executive vice-president for corporate relations for Ford was asked about how the law affects Ford and the UAW. Pestillo responded:

> I think the National Labor Relations Act plays a very small role in our lives. We've got a long history and culture that allows us to operate and I think that's an important distinction. We're not burdened by it, quite frankly. We don't recklessly violate it, mind you, but with a 100,000 people, over the course of a year you won't see NLRB charges to Ford Motor company.[9]

Management, in these examples, does not keep information from the union, although they may have the legal right to do so. They often do not assert their legal right to make decisions regarding the direction of the business free from union "interference," although they may legally do this. They do not use the negotiation process to make proposals that the union must find unacceptable, as they may, force a strike, and then exercise their legal rights to replace those strikers.

Rather, the parties recognize the legitimacy of one another. The company not only recognizes the union in the legal sense, but also in the practical sense, as the true representative of its employee-stakeholders. As will be seen, the parties that have successful relationships do not interact through the legal system. They negotiate based on their respective interests. Although not all of the parties have reached the same level of cooperation, all of these relationships are characterized by mutual respect for the legitimacy of the other party and by reliance on negotiation rather than legal confrontation.

Ford Sharonville (Ohio) Transmission Plant and the United Auto Workers.[10] The Ford Sharonville transmission plant, near Cincinnati, employs 2,000 people. The plant manufactures two automatic transmissions: the E40D, fully electronic, described as "the newest and best in its field;" and the C6, an older type. The transmissions go in F-series trucks and Econoline vans.

In the early 1980s and as late as 1986, Ford had intended to close the facility. For years the plant management and the union at Ford Sharonville had a traditional, nonparticipative relationship. The parties realized, however, that they would need to change in order to save the plant and the jobs of the employees. The change in the relationship started in 1979, with a National Letter of Understanding negotiated between Ford and the UAW. The purpose was to make the company and the union aware of different options for ordering their relationship. In 1980, a joint Employee Involvement (EI) steering committee formed at Sharonville. The company members of the steering committee were the plant manager, the industrial relations manager, two area managers within the plant, and the quality control manager. The union members included the entire bargaining committee.

In 1981, joint EI coordinators were appointed and EI pilot groups started among hourly and salaried employees. In 1983, EI area subcommittees formed from middle management and the plant floor committee. In 1985, the first self-directed work team was piloted. That was the same year that the plant was awarded the E40D transmission.

After the E40D award, the skilled trades (electrical, hydraulic, machine repair, and tool makers) established cross-functional teams to launch new equipment. The teams were provided with eighty hours of training in order that each trade could learn the basics of the other trades. Although this was a voluntary program for the skilled trades, over 90 percent of the skilled tradespeople in the plant participated.

Local management and the union together determined the selection process for staffing new teams, posted jobs, and explained expectations to those who volunteered. There would be a single classification for manufacturing—manufacturing technician. Each technician was given three weeks of training before being assigned to a team; two weeks of technical training and one week of instruction on working in teams. Additional training was provided after people were assigned to teams. This training included roles and responsibilities of team members, problem solving, and conflict management.

The manufacturing team consists of eight to twelve manufacturing technicians, an hourly team coordinator (who, at that time, was paid an additional 10 cents per hour and was elected by the team, with some encouragement to rotate among team members), and a salaried advisor (formerly a supervisor but now more of a coach). The manufacturing technicians are paid, according to knowledge, up to four or five levels. The team reports to the superintendent. If there are disagreements, they go to the plant manager, and then, if necessary, to the plant manager

The technicians are responsible for production, scheduling lunch and relief, and vacations. They work with the advisor to obtain approval for overtime. They schedule overtime, determine training needs, and train others as appropriate, decide daily job assignments and rotations, and ensure proper coverage of critical jobs. The team coordinator chairs team meetings, attends appropriate safety, quality, and other plant meetings.

The team process was reviewed in 1990 and monitored thereafter. In 1991, it was determined that additional training was needed, especially for the advisors.

Training is important at Ford, as it provides a flexible structure for consistency. A total of 151 personal development courses can be taken at the plant, with all the courses designed at the national level.

The results have been dramatic. Between 1988 and 1992, there was a 40 percent drop in first-time visits for medical attention and a 53 percent improvement in quality. Total safety costs have improved by 57 percent since 1979. Sharonville, a plant that ten years ago was slated for closing, recently won an internal bid for transmission work that will keep the plant in operation at least through the year 2000.

At Ford Sharonville, there appears to be a blurring of the line between hourly workers and supervisors. Indeed, the team, staffed by hourly workers, does much of the work scheduling that has traditionally been the prerogative of supervisors. The company has been quite willing to share its management prerogatives with the union, although the law obviously does not require them to do so. When the relationship between the company and the union is one of trust, the law tends not to be an issue.

New United Manufacturing Company (NUMMI) and the UAW[11.] The New United Manufacturing Company (NUMMI) is a joint venture of General Motors and Toyota, producing small cars in an old GM plant in Fremont, California. NUMMI grew out of the deep recession in the early 1980s, during which California's number of auto plants dropped from 8 to 1. Among those closed was the GM plant in Fremont.

In 1983, GM and Toyota established a joint venture to run the former GM plant according to Toyota's production system. The plant had one of the worst disciplinary and grievance records in the GM system. NUMMI management had doubts about dealing with the Fremont workforce, but decided to establish a "win-win" relationship. As a gesture of good faith, they agreed to hire back the old workforce and to pay wages and benefits comparable to those received by UAW-represented employees in the auto industry. In the event of a downturn in sales, management agreed not to lay off any employees until management salaries were reduced, subcontracted work was brought back in, and then only if the long-term financial viability of the firm was at stake. They have kept that pledge. The union, for its part, agreed to the Toyota team concept, to give up traditional work rules, and to become co-responsible with the company for improving quality and productivity.

In order to accomplish this, a culture change was required. The militant shop committee was rehired, as a company commitment to working with the representatives of the employees. This committee participated in staffing the facility. The first several months were spent interviewing for team leaders (foreman equivalents). Once the plant was up and running, the UAW was given the right to slow down the line at any time if there were quality problems. A job security clause was incorporated into the contract so people would not think they would lose their jobs if they made suggestions. Production was slowly increased until the line could be run at full without sacrificing quality.

The company has been willing to involve employees in almost every phase of the operation. Typical management symbols like a separate cafeteria and parking spaces are gone. With 4,000 employees, only twenty-two grievances had been submitted for outside resolution after

ten years. There were twenty-two grievances submitted for outside resolution each month under the former GM management. The contract
provides employees with job security and "top of the industry" wages,
which, from the point of view of the union, was an essential trade-off
for successful team efforts to increase quality and productivity.

Miller Brewing and UAW Local 2308.[12] In October of 1990, Miller
Brewing decided to open a plant in Trenton, Ohio, near Cincinnati. The
company wanted a high-commitment, high-performance, multicultural
work environment with work teams exemplifying self-management,
continuous improvement, and operational flexibility. The company,
however, also assumed that the plant would be organized, as the brewing industry has traditionally been unionized. Thus, the company recognized the UAW as the bargaining representative of its Trenton
employees.

Operationally, although management retained certain responsibilities, there was union involvement at every level, including weekly staff
meetings. The roles of labor and management were redefined. The parties developed two documents. The first, the traditional collective bargaining agreement, was expected to be constant during its life. The
second, the *Trenton Brewery Operating Guidelines,* included procedures the parties expected to change to ensure that the plant was
responsive to customers and the workforce. The parties developed an
Issue Resolution Procedure, which permitted all members of the workforce and their team managers, on a rotating basis, to resolve problems
and set plantwide policies.

Another structure, the Policy Review Board, takes plant management and local union interests into account, gathers data, and formu-
lates policy independent of the corporate office and the international
union. An extensive communication network was developed which
included e-mail for every employee, daily information meetings, morning production planning meetings, weekly communications meetings,
monthly three-shift meetings, and an annual plant conference, for
which the plant shuts down for a full day, with outsiders making presentations.

In terms of plant performance, the relationship seems to be successful. The plant experienced a very fast start-up. In October of 1993, it
was producing about 40,000 barrels per day; it was 50 percent more
productive than other Miller operations.

Miller Brewing could have exercised its legal rights to resist the union; it chose not to do so. Rather, the company accepted the legitimacy of the union and determined to negotiate with the union as the representative of its employees. The results have been excellent for all concerned.

BellSouth and Communications Workers of America.[13] The relationship between BellSouth and the Communication Workers of America (CWA) has historically been conflict laden. After a series of strikes in the 1970s, the CWA and BellSouth leadership decided that more could be done by working together than by airing differences in the old way. The parties changed the grievance procedure to permit a union steward to talk to a supervisor without writing a formal grievance. The parties decided that any such grievance settlements would be nonbinding and nonprecedent setting. This helped to resolve problems at the lowest level, creating dialogue instead of confrontation.

After a strike in 1983 over health care, BellSouth and the CWA established a joint committee on health care, moving toward managed care with union involvement. CWA locals had direct input on hospitals to be included in the network. As a result, health care was not an issue in the negotiations of 1986, 1989, or 1992.

The parties then moved to other issues. Given the rapidly changing competitive environment in the communications industry, BellSouth and the CWA determined that the traditional collective bargaining relationship of periodic contract negotiations with a voluminous, inflexible agreement was no longer appropriate. In 1991, at the beginning of the current contract, the parties agreed to establish, on a trial basis, a continuous standing bargaining committee. It was the charge of this committee to deal with festering work rule matters that had traditionally been put aside during bargaining, in order to get the contract completed.

Discussions in the new committee were low-profile, low-key, and nonthreatening. No demands were made. Seating at the meetings was interspersed rather than each party sitting on its side of the table. No bulletins were issued on the progress of the negotiations that could cause constituents to put pressure on their representative. The parties found that they were more honestly communicating needs and identifying issues. Thus the parties will again bargain this way when they negotiate their next three-year agreement.

Despite the good will of the parties, there continue to be points of disagreement. BellSouth has been reducing employment and requiring remaining employees to work harder. Workforce reductions have led to additional grievances. This reminds us that while there is much that brings the parties together, there is also much that continues to divide labor and management.

Although the relationship has not been smooth, as would be expected given the uncertainty in the telecommunications industry, the parties have not stood on the legal rights to eschew negotiations during the term of the agreement. They have moved into a problem-solving mode rather than a rights mode.

Ciba-Geigy, Mackintosh, Texas and the Oil, Chemical and Atomic Workers Union.[14] Ciba-Geigy built its Mackintosh facility in 1952. The plant was organized by OCAW in 1956. The plant has 1,332 employees, of which 700 are represented by the OCAW.

The first twenty-five years of the relationship were contentious, including a strike in 1974. The plant had experienced frequent layoffs and indifferent hiring. It was losing patents and was adversely affected by the bad public image of the chemical industry.

With the survival of the plant at stake, a new site manager was assigned to Mackintosh in 1980. He removed management perks, expressed a concern for the environment, and moved towards improving the labor-management relationship through employee involvement. Mackintosh is now a leader in health, safety, and environment, through the efforts of its joint committee dedicated to these ends. There also is a joint labor-management council in place with which the company shares information and agrees on training. Productivity has improved, and there have been no layoffs at Mackintosh since 1984.

National Steel and the United Steelworkers of America.[15] National Steel is the fourth largest steel company in the United States. It is 72 percent owned by NKK of Japan. National Steel is a fully integrated steel company, with such major customers as General Motors, Ford, Chrysler, Toyota, Nissan, Honda, and Del Monte. The company has experienced difficult times in the last two decades, with employment dropping from 25,000 in 1968 to 10,000 in 1993. During the 1980s, demand for steel was declining at the same time that competition was increasing. This decline in demand was caused to a large extent by the rise of steel substitutes, such as aluminum for cans and plastics in automobiles. At the same time, competition was increasing; imported steel currently accounts for 30 percent of the market in the United States.

Given these changes in the steel market, National decided in 1983 that the traditional multiemployer bargaining structure no longer suited it. They no longer wished their competitors, such as US Steel and Bethlehem, negotiating for them, and they no longer wished to deal with the United Steelworkers through an adversarial relationship. Thus, in 1984, National withdrew from multiemployer bargaining to pursue a cooperative bargaining approach.

The collective bargaining relationship between National Steel and the Steelworkers, prior to 1984, was described as "open warfare" by a union representative.[16] In 1984, however, the company approached the union in an attempt to change the relationship and to build mutual trust. The parties established study committees of staff representatives and company officials, with support from international union headquarters and corporate headquarters for financial and benefits expertise. Rules were established. The committee would discuss issues, but these would not be negotiating sessions. The company would provide all information requested, eschewing claims of confidentiality. In return, the union agreed not to reveal it. Each side selected an outside consultant, which had to be approved by the other party.

The parties met on issues involving safety and health, employment security, benefits, insurance, pensions, and profit sharing. Eventually, the cooperation became so deeply embedded that one "could not tell who is union and who is management."[17] The program survived a scare in 1985, when the company requested concessions, but the parties worked through it.

The committee system was carried over into bargaining. The parties strengthened it in the 1989 agreement, and in 1993 they negotiated a six-year agreement. The 1993 agreement includes a formal cooperative partnership, which includes the president and chief operating officer of the company, and the international president of the union. This partnership group does strategic planning for how the cooperative process should go forward. It is a structured approach at plant level where leaders steer the process down to the shop floor level, where foreman and stewards are the leaders.

What have been the results of this change? Employees have guaranteed employment security except in a complete shutdown of a facility or with the approval of the Steelworkers international president. The union is committed to productivity improvements, including craft combinations; indeed, in Michigan, the parties reduced the classifications to two crafts, mechanics and electricians. Employees have been given a stake in the business through profit-sharing and gainsharing and an intellectual stake through the cooperative partnership.

From the financial viewpoint, employment costs stayed basically flat from 1986 through 1993, while productivity increased. In 1984, productivity was 5.5 person hours per ton; by 1993, this had been reduced to less than 4 person-hours per ton. Productivity gainsharing was $25 million in 1992. When there were profits in 1987-89, there was also profitsharing—$40 million in 1988.

In 1991, the company went to the union asking for help. The union responded by reducing costs $100 million in the second half of 1991. National Steel was the only major steel company that was profitable in 1991. As for the employees, when the rest of the industry laid off an average of 10 percent of its workforce in 1991, National Steel laid off only 150 employees, all of whom had not been employed the one year required to earn employment security rights.

Finally, it is interesting to note that National Steel is the most heavily unionized major steel company in the United States; all of the office workers are unionized. The union attributes this to a neutrality pledge by National Steel. The company recognizes the right of the union to exist.

Summary

Consistent with the subthemes raised in the previous chapter, both parties in these relationships eschew reliance on their legal rights. There is no claim on the part of the employer that some subjects are nonmandatory or out of bounds, despite their legal right to do so. These parties view labor relations in a problem-solving and issue-oriented framework rather than as a battle of relative rights.

Employment Relations Innovation in Nonunion Firms

As noted in the previous chapter, the most salient aspect of employment relations since the 1970s has been the rise of the nonunion employment relations system. All of these systems, however, could fairly be described as "top down." The employer, acting on its own, would determine terms and conditions of employment, such as pay and benefit systems, performance appraisal systems, career paths, and promotional criteria. While human resources departments would take into account such factors as market trends, the actions of comparable organizations, or fairness, it was also true that such systems lacked one important feature of the unionized sector—a formal, recognized mechanism for obtaining employee views on various matters.

As competition increased in the 1980s, it became increasingly important for firms to tap the expertise of all of their employees, production and clerical as well as supervisory and management. Indeed, it soon became clear that improvements in the production process of many goods and services could be made without substantial capital outlays by relying on the knowledge and suggestions of those who were most intimately familiar with the production process—employees who were actually doing it.

Firms also began to realize that management did not always know the wishes of employees. High morale and job satisfaction often required knowing what employees wanted, not only in wages and benefits, but also with respect to such matters as equipment, production processes, and safety.

Thus, some nonunion firms began to create processes to formally obtain employee input on a variety of matters. As discussed in the previous chapter, these plans and processes often did raise legal questions. Were the companies that established them in violation of the National Labor Relations Act? If not, would the NLRB be condoning structures that might be designed to prevent employees from choosing an independent representative? If so, was the legal system denying nonunion employers the right to consult with their employees who did not choose union representation? The cases in this section discuss different forms of innovative, nontraditional employment relations systems in nonunion companies.[18]

Donnelly Corporation.[19] The Donnelly Corporation, which was founded in 1905, is an automotive supplier of interior and exterior mirrors and encapsulated modular windows. The company also supplies glass components for appliances. It has annual sales of about $300 million and employs 2,600 workers worldwide. Two thousand employees are in twelve facilities in western Michigan. The company also has facilities in Ireland, Arizona, and Kentucky, and joint ventures in Colorado, Tennessee, and California.

The company has been a model of innovative employment relations for forty years. It adopted a Scanlon Plan (profit- and gainsharing plan) in 1952. The principle behind the plan was to encourage employees to help make improvements and to share the results of those improvements. In the late 1960s, the company went to a team concept, eliminating time clocks and putting all employees on salary within the constraints of the Fair Labor Standards Act.

In the late 1960s, the company created an "equity structure," which is now a "representative structure." It incorporates a hierarchy of committees, with the Donnelly committee at the top. The structure processes all wages, benefits, and terms and conditions of employment and provides a safety net for the grievance process and a guarantee that people have a voice in the development of policies that affect them. The structure operates on the principle of unanimous agreement, which is really a system of full consultation.

An excellent example of how the Donnelly process works was provided by three employees from the modular systems department, which produces two kinds of windows for one of the domestic auto companies. According to the employees, the department was a poor place to work in 1989-90. There were obvious distinctions between desirable and undesirable jobs, costs were high, yields were low, and quality was poor. The team leadership decided that a change was necessary. They believed it was important for people to know the entire process in the department. Thus, on the initiative of the representatives, all teams were taken off-site for training. The production system was redesigned and the representatives made sure that the support systems and reward systems fit the new operating system. After redesign, cross-sectional teams were created to address issues and concerns from the redesign. Since implementation started in mid 1991, there has been a 65 percent reduction in customer returns and scrap, a 25 percent improvement in productivity, and a substantial improvement in the work climate.

A Delta (change) Continuous Improvement Plan was also initiated. Teams were empowered to make decisions and involve others if necessary. The team analyzes problems and implements solutions. A team may solicit help from customers (auto companies) and suppliers. Before Delta, average production was pieces 471 per shift with five people on line; after Delta, yield was 526 pieces per shift with four people. The yield (good parts) is 98.6 percent.

Herman Miller Corporation.[20] Herman Miller is an office furniture manufacturer headquartered in western Michigan. The firm employs 5,700 people worldwide. Employee participation at Herman Miller began in the 1950s with a Scanlon Plan. The major thrust of the Herman Miller system lies in its values. The company believes that every employee is "authentic," and that all employees are entitled to be treated with courtesy and good manners. Operationally, the company has moved from a hierarchically structured organization to what it calls an "adaptable relational organization." Currently, annual corporate planning involves every employee. Every employee with one year of tenure is given stock through profit-sharing. Employees with two years service are provided with a "silver parachute" designed to protect them from unjust discharge or job reassignment in the event of a takeover. The "parachute" provides one year of wage continuation and maintenance of health benefits. The cash compensation of the chief executive officer is capped at twenty times the average salary of the manufacturing employee average.

As regards day-to-day workplace issues, the company has work teams, with team leaders selected by management based on the competencies and work required to lead a group of people. For issues of discharge, there is an internal appeals board made up of five members chosen by the employees from a board of ten. There is a suggestion review board, selected by management, which follows up on all employee suggestions. The suggestor is included in the follow-up, and the suggestor may appeal to management if his or her idea is not accepted.

Delta Airlines.[21] Delta believes that its success is based on the relationship between management and personnel, and the flexibility this provides. From Delta's perspective, the essential components to developing a strong relationship are cooperation, employee participation, and treating employees with dignity. The company holds personnel meetings every twelve to eighteen months. During 1993, Delta CEO Ron Allen visited all major cities and held town hall meetings to impart management's vision of the future and address employee concerns. All senior management frequently visit personnel in operating areas and volunteer to work side-by-side with employees loading bags, cleaning airplanes, and providing customer service.

When severe competition in the airline industry required Delta to implement cost reductions, including a 5 percent pay reduction and several changes to their benefit package, the relationship was tested but employees were ultimately supportive because of previous education and communication. As part of the cost reduction plan, a president's team was established to evaluate employee suggestions. There were 20,000 suggestions, resulting in $50 million in actual savings.

In maintenance and technical operations, Delta has a technical evaluation committee composed of employees who leave their current job assignments to analyze technical and mechanical systems and to think of ways to reengineer processes. In addition, other employees also submit suggestions to the committee. The company also has corporate safety teams for large operational areas, tuition assistance, a destination program for language learning, and a development program for managerial and process skills. In Delta's view, improvement of worker-management relations is a function of each enterprise; each corporation and their employees need to explore what works best.

Coca-Cola, USA.[22] At Coca-Cola's Nashua, New Hampshire plant, the company has been implementing total quality work design efforts (TQWD)—a process of changing work to improve productivity and quality, create more efficiency and shared responsibility, and provide better jobs. Although the Nashua plant is the premier syrup plant in the system, the employees and management wished to improve. The company taught people how to be involved in the business and provided a shared vision and a common framework. Training was offered to employees in interpersonal skills, teams skills, meeting management skills, and business skills. Following this, employee groups undertook an analysis of the business, technical, and social environment, with the customer as the focal point. Seven committees were created: public service; branch activities; budget; associate motivation and policy enforcement; health and safety; continuous improvement; and training and development.

Texas Instruments, Inc.[23] Texas Instruments has developed a team concept in its microcircuit board shop and in its manufacture of infrared imaging devices. The microcircuit board goes into the seeker selection section of the HARM missile. Until 1990, management told the shop employees what they would do each day and how many boards they would build. There was no cross-training and no way that the employees could educate themselves in other shop processes. In general, employees had no idea how the shop ran, and they believed their input was not valued.

In 1990, the shop was organized into seven process teams, each building a product from start to finish. The teams cross- train each other. As a result, absenteeism or vacation scheduling do not shut the shop down. The team has the authority to manage day-to-day operations, assumes all supervisory responsibilities, such as approving labor, tracking the support of other teams, initiating corrective action on performance issues, staffing, and managing overtime, which includes trying to reduce it. The team does action plans based on production trends tracked. As a result, between December 1990 and December 1993, cycle time was reduced by 64 percent, quality increased 20 percent, and production staffing dropped 46 percent, all with improved employee self-esteem.

A second example is the "diamond turning point team." The team produces optical components for the Texas Instruments defense systems and electronics group, using a gem quality diamond to produce an optical grade surface on the infrared imaging piece parts. In June, 1992, the department implemented a five-star point team: the five star points were administrative, quality control, methods and tooling, safety, and production control. Each star point acts as liaison to the rest of team. Quality has improved, with defects dropping from 375 in 1991 to 35 in 1993. Cycle time is down from six days to one day, improving on-time delivery. The method improvement program lets workers make changes in the processes. Workers ideas generated savings of $65,000 in 1993.

D.D. Williamson and Co.[24] D.D.Williamson, in Louisville, is part of an international group of small companies that manufacturers caramel colors. The firm has 800 customers and a 40 percent market share. This nonunion firm uses teams and employee involvement. All employees are members of quality teams. There are also multifunctional product-oriented teams. One team generated $70,000 in savings by solving an effluent problem. An information systems team put in a new computer system for the company. The company invests heavily in training and education. Prior to 1987, the average employee received approximately ten hours of training per year. Since 1987, the average employee yearly receives sixty to eighty hours of training. The plant shuts down one day per quarter to facilitate various kinds of training. The firm's self-managed work teams allowed the company to replace supervisors with team leaders, who have the authority to hire, fire, and rotate workers. Each associate has a $374 voucher that can be spent in any plant-related way he or she wishes, either individually or by combining with the vouchers of other employees. All employees visit and make presentations to customers; they also must make a presentation at their own plant when they return.

Lantech, Inc.[25] Lantech, Inc. is a Louisville firm that manufactures and markets stretch packaging machinery. Established in 1972, the company had $40 million in sales in 1992. The firm employs 280 people. Its main customers are Fortune 500 companies who use the packaging to wrap their product. Benefits provided by the company include full health and life insurance, tuition advances, a computer loan program, a four-day, ten-hour workweek, flexible hours, and internal placement. The company has an open door policy, with each employee having the capability of sending voice mail to anybody in the firm, including the owner. There is a complete sharing of information. Once per month, there is an all-employee meeting on the financial condition of the firm, orders, and company strategy. There are also monthly division meetings.

Summary

The seven examples brought forth indicate the range of innovation that nonunion firms have initiated without the constraints of the law. With the exception of Donnelly Corporation, and in that case, only in a minor way, none of the innovations focused on wages, hours, and working conditions. The major thrust of these innovations seems to be to change the organization of work so that workers can contribute to the production process and the success of the firm. The team processes that have been established not only provide workers enhanced self-esteem and job satisfaction, they also have made substantial and measurable contributions to firm performance.

Conclusion

This chapter does not purport to be a complete analysis of labor-management cooperation in the United States. In that regard, we are aware that the presentations at the hearing were likely to be biased toward success stories, as only those successful programs would be willing to go public. The purpose of this volume, however, is not to analyze the reasons for success and failure of innovative labor-management programs. That has been done elsewhere.[26] Rather, the purpose of this volume is to demonstrate the range of relationships possible under the current industrial relations legal structure in the United States. Thus, these cases should be viewed as evidence of the existence of such structures, not as evidence of their long- term success.

Indeed, it should be observed that not every relationship featured was an unqualified success. The presenters discussing the relationship between Lyondell and the OCAW, for example, freely admitted that the parties have not had the success they would have liked, as they cannot agree on the level of the union's participation.

Is is also conceded that such cooperative programs are not the only means to productivity; traditional labor relations can also lead to productivity gains.[27] The point, however, is that a firm can be productive through cooperation as well as through conflict, suggesting that the choice of labor relations models, per se, does not necessarily determine productivity.

Overall, three observations seem especially relevant at this point. First, the general role of government can be that of a facilitator of labor-management cooperation. While it is clear that overall government policy, at the national level, seems decidedly neutral on the matter of labor-management relations, government can facilitate innovation and cooperation if it so desires.

Second, it is clear that legalism and the law play but a small role in these innovative, cooperative relationships. The parties do not assert legal rights vis-a-vis each other (for example, the employer's right to withhold information), and they do not interact through the courts and the NLRB. Rather, they negotiate and behave in a problem-solving mode.

Third, it appears that the National Labor Relations Act has not been a barrier to innovation and cooperation in nonunion firms. The corporations discussed in this chapter have all created ways to involve their employees without necessarily running afoul of the law.

Overall, then, the lesson seems to be that if management is truly interested in treating its employees well and involving its employees in the production process, the law does not prevent them from doing so. Management makes the determination, and management has a choice. The implications of this will be discussed in the concluding chapter.

NOTES

1. It seems fair to say that from the period 1935-47, the NLRA was designed to encourage workers to unionize. The law, however, was neutral as regard the nature of that collective bargaining relationship, once established.

2. *Transcript of the Hearing of the Committee on the Future of Worker-Management Relations,* Louisville, Kentucky, September 22, 1993, pp. 17-24.

3. *Transcript of the Hearing of the Commission on the Future of Worker-Management Relations,* Louisville, Kentucky, September 22, 1993, pp. 106-21.

4. *Transcript of the Hearing of the Commission on the Future of Worker-Management Relations,* Louisville, Kentucky, September 22, 1993, pp.73-87.

5. In traditional bargaining, each side makes notes during negotiations that it keeps for its records. Such notes may be used as evidence in any subsequent arbitration over the agreement. The absence of notes means that the only record of the negotiations is joint, as opposed to creating two partisan, perhaps conflicting, records.

6. *Transcript of the Hearing of the Commission on the Future of Worker-Management Relations,* Atlanta, Georgia, January 11, 944, pp. 89-100.

7. *Transcript of the Hearing of the Commission on the Future of Worker-Management Relations,* Houston, Texas, February 11, 1994, pp. 41-52.

8. *Transcript of the Hearing of the Commission on the Future of Worker-Management Relations,* Washington, DC, July 28, 1993, pp. 160-212.

9. *Transcript of the Hearing of the Commission on the Future of Worker-Management Relations,* Washington, DC, July 28, 1993, pp. 48-49.

10. *Transcript of the Hearing of the Commission on the Future of Worker-Management Relations,* Washington, DC, July 28, 1993, pp. 17-43.

11. *Transcript of the Hearing of the Commission on the Future of Worker-Management Relations,* San Jose, California, January 27, 1994, pp. 92-114.

12. *Transcript of the Hearing of the Commission on the Future of Worker-Management Relations,* East Lansing, Michigan, October 13, 1993, pp. 31-41.

13. *Transcript of the Hearing of the Commission on the Future of Worker-Management Relations,* Atlanta, Georgia, January 11, 1993, pp. 72-83.

14. *Transcript of the Hearing of the Commission on the Future of Worker-Management Relations,* Houston, Texas, February 11, 1994, pp. 124-42.

15. *Transcript of the Hearing of the Commission on the Future of Worker-Management Relations,* Washington, DC, September 15, 1993, pp. 6-55.

16. *Transcript of the Hearing of the Commission on the Future of Worker-Management Relations,* Washington, DC, September 15, 1993, p. 16.

17.*Transcript of the Hearing of the Commission on the Future of Worker-Management Relations,* Washington, DC, September 15, 1993, p. 23.

18. The examples listed here are not the only ones that were brought to the attention of the Dunlop Commission. Other nonunion firms testifying about innovative employee relations were Federal Express, Intel, VCW Corporation (Kansas City, Kansas), and Wil-Burt Corporation (Norville, Ohio).

19. *Transcript of the Hearing of the Commission on the Future of Worker-Management Relations,* East Lansing, Michigan, October 13, 1993, pp. 55-75.

20. *Transcript of the Hearing of the Commission on the Future of Worker-Management Relations,* East Lansing, Michigan, October 13, 1993, pp. 41-54.

21. *Transcript of the Hearing of the Commission on the Future of Worker-Management Relations,* Atlanta, Georgia, January 11, 1993, pp. 83-89.

22. *Transcript of the Hearing of the Commission on the Future of Worker-Management Relations,* Atlanta, Georgia, January 11, 1994, pp. 101-17.

23. *Transcript of the Hearing of the Commission on the Future of Worker-Management Relations,* Atlanta, Georgia, January 11, 1994, pp. 101-08.

24. *Transcript of the Hearing of the Commission on the Future of Worker-Management Relations,* Louisville, Kentucky, September 22, 1993, pp. 164-71.

25. *Transcript of the Hearing of the Commission on the Future of Worker-Management Relations,* Louisville, Kentucky, September 22, 1993, pp. 172-80.

26. See, for example, Gershenfeld (1987); and Cooke (1990).

27. See, for example, Voos (1987); Cooke (1990, 1992, 1994); and Levine and D'Andrea Tyson (1990).

CHAPTER 4

Impairment of Workers' Rights of Choice

The essence of the National Labor Relations Act is employee choice. The basic rights in the Act are enumerated in Section 7, which gives employees the right to form, join, or assist labor organizations, and engage in concerted activity for mutual aid and protection and for the purposes of collective bargaining; it also gives employees the right to refrain from engaging in such activity. If employees choose union representation for collective bargaining purposes, the Act requires the employer to bargain with the union selected, in essence permitting the manifestation of the right of self-organization.

Most of the National Labor Relations Act is designed to effectuate this choice. The unfair labor practices in the NLRA are, to a large extent, designed to prevent infringements on worker choice by employers and by unions. Section 8(a)(1), a general prohibition on employers, prevents employer restraint, interference, and coercion with this right. Sections 8(a)(2) through 8(a)(5) constitute prohibitions on specific employer activity that Congress believed impaired the right of employees to choose. Section 8(a)(2) prevents employer domination of or assistance to a labor organization, as Congress believed that employees should not be required to consider an organization that was not independent of the employer.[1] Section 8(a)(3) prevents employer discrimination in terms or conditions of employment to encourage or discourage membership in a labor organization. Section 8(a)(4) prevents employer discrimination for giving testimony or filing charges under the Act. Section 8(a)(5) requires the employer to bargain with the union duly selected by the employees. Section 8(b)(1) of the Act extends this prohibition on impairing employee choice to unions, preventing them from restraining or coercing employees in their rights under Section 7.

Article 10 creates a full enforcement mechanism for these (and the other) unfair labor practices under the Act. It gives the NLRB the right to take evidence, subpoena witnesses, and issue appropriate orders. Courts of appeals are involved, either through an NLRB enforcement order or through an appeal by a party "aggrieved" by an NLRB order. Parties may, in turn, request Supreme Court review of court of appeals decisions.

Section 9 implements the notion of choice by authorizing the NLRB to conduct a representation election to determine whether an appropriate unit of employees wish to be represented for collective purposes. The Board will conduct such an election once there is a "showing of substantial interest"—when at least 30 percent of the employees in an appropriate unit have signed cards authorizing a union to represent them or have otherwise demonstrated that they wish to be represented by a union. The Board also has the authority to determine an appropriate unit, i.e., which employees have a sufficient "community of interest" to be included together in a rational bargaining unit. This Board authority facilitates the employee choice process by not limiting the choice process to all employees in particular facility or location. Smaller but occupationally or economically rational groups of employees may also make that choice.[2]

The Legal Situation

Observations on the Choice Process

A key component of the choice mechanism is the NLRB representation election campaign. Upon a finding of substantial interest, the Board will attempt to schedule an election to be held within thirty days. With questions often being raised about the composition of the bargaining unit and other such matters, 80 percent of all elections are held within three months of the representation petition.[3] During this period between petition and election, a campaign is conducted, during which the employer and the union each present their views on the matter of unionization of the unit.

As noted in chapter 2, the law of union organizing, based on principles of free speech and property rights, has evolved over the last forty years so as to provide employers with a great deal of freedom to present their point of view at the workplace as long as they do not explicitly threaten, restrain, or coerce employees. This includes the right to require employees, individually or in groups, to listen to the employer's point of view on union matters. On the other hand, also based on principles of property rights, the law permits employers to generally bar unions from their property, and to limit employee campaigning for the union to break periods and lunch periods. Unions, for their part, are generally limited to literature distribution on the nearest public property, home visits, telephone calls, and voluntary meetings (Block and Wolkinson 1986; Block, Wolkinson, and Kuhn 1988).

Given such rights, an employer who is so inclined has the capability and the right to campaign against the union daily and constantly during the election campaign, exposing the employees to its point of view as much as it wishes and in whatever forums it wishes. In other words, the workplace is not a neutral forum where the costs and benefits of unionization are discussed openly and freely.[4] Rather, because of the nature of employer property rights, the workplace is a location where one point of view—the employer's—is presented almost exclusively. As the workplace is the only opportunity for all employees to gather together and discuss unionism, the result is that the employer has a near monopoly on access to employees during the election campaign.

Although the unfair labor practices in the Act are designed to prevent employers from interfering with employee rights of self-organization, the procedures under the NLRA for resolving disputes over the appropriateness of the bargaining unit permit employers who are so inclined to delay the election and extend the campaign, permitting them to further benefit from their access advantage among employees.

In addition, the nonpunitive remedial philosophy in the NLRA allows employers to aggressively explore their rights under the Act to oppose unionization. Because the property rights of employers permit them to take action and maintain that action pending a final disposition of the case, including exhaustion of all appeals, employees who have been the victims of an alleged unfair labor practice must bear the burden of the delay resulting from the time it takes to process the case and the appeals.[5]

Even if the employer is ultimately found to have committed an unfair labor practice, it must only reinstate the employee with back pay less interim earnings. There are no additional punitive damages assessed. In other words, the employer is not "punished" for its violation, thereby lessening the cost of violating the NLRA as compared to what the cost would be with a punitive remedial system.[6]

Employees of an employer who aggressively opposes unionization may be reluctant to openly support unionization for fear of being discharged and having to undergo a long and somewhat uncertain legal process without employment. In addition, such a concern could discourage other employees from supporting unionization. In this way, the right of employees to choose unionization could be impaired.

When Employees Select a Union

Where employees select a union to represent them, after all challenges and objections to the election are resolved, the union is "certified" as the representative of the employees. At that time, the question of representation is considered settled for one year. The Board will not accept a decertification petition nor any employer claim that it doubts the union's majority status. The purpose of this one-year hiatus in raising the representation question is to give the parties the opportunity to establish a collective bargaining relationship.

It is the legal obligation of the employer to bargain in good faith with the union. This is a straightforward extension of the choice principle—if employees select representation, the employer has a legal obligation to honor that choice. Although both parties must bargain in good faith, neither side is required to agree to anything. In the event the employer is found in violation of the Act, the absence of Board authority to impose terms and conditions of employment means that it can only issue a cease-and-desist order, essentially directing the employer to do what it should have done originally—bargain. Moreover, such an order may not be final until after all appeals are exhausted, which may take up to two years. Again, the employees must bear the burden of the employer's appeals.[7]

Finally, both sides may engage in self-help in the event there is no agreement on a contract. The employees, through their union, may strike, and the employer may lock out the employees. The employer's right to self-help also extends to permanently replacing the strikers, if it so desires.[8]

When a Union is Not Selected

When a union is not selected and all objections and challenges are resolved, as is the case when the union is selected, another election cannot be held for another year. The principle is that the employees and the employer should be relieved of the pressure of an organizing campaign. During that period, although the employees may continue to support the union, the union may not picket the employer for recognition or organization.

Summary

The foregoing is a brief overview of the law covering employee choice of whether or not to be represented collectively by a union. How have these rights been effectuated in practice? The next section will use the testimony at the Dunlop Commission hearings to demonstrate how employee rights are affected by the exercise of employer rights to resist unionization.

Employer Behavior and Employee Choice

As discussed in chapter 2 and in the previous section of this chapter, the principle of employee freedom of choice of collective or individual representation is at the heart of the National Labor Relations Act. The Dunlop Commission heard a great deal of testimony from employees and union representatives suggesting that the choice mechanism can be distorted by employers who are so inclined.

The purpose of this section of the chapter is to use the testimony before the Dunlop Commission to illustrate how the National Labor Relations Act, which was enacted to protect employee choice in representation, can be used to actually impair employee choice. The material in this section of the chapter was taken directly from the transcripts of the Commission hearings. Although we had no reason to disbelieve what was said before the Commission, we believed it was necessary to obtain some independent corroboration of the statements where possible, given the statements that were made regarding employer behavior. Thus, in all cases in which the testimony indicated that the employer had been found by the NLRB to have committed an unfair labor practice, we found the case in the reporting services. For all cases that were located, it was found that the employee or the union representative had testified accurately about the charge, the facts, and the outcome.[9] This gave us sufficient confidence in the veracity of the testimony to use it in this chapter.

Given our decision to use the testimony, we decided to omit all identifiers, despite the fact that in all cases except one, the individuals who testified provided their names and identified the company involved. We have omitted the names of the employers because the purpose of this volume is not to criticize or accuse individual companies of wrongdoing. Rather, our purpose is to demonstrate a systemic problem under our laws—to show that any employer so inclined has the ability to behave in this way. The names of the employees were omitted because we were concerned about their employers being able to identify them.

This section of the chapter is divided into two subsections. The first addresses impairment of employee choice during the organizing and election process; the second addresses impairment of the employees' right to bargain collectively after they have made the choice to be represented by a union.

Employer Behavior vis-a-vis Employee Attempts at Organization

The control the employer has over the workplace and the make-whole (nonpunitive) principle of the remedial structure of the NLRA provide an incentive for employers who are so inclined to operate on the margin of the law. Penalties are mild and the benefits, in terms of discouraging employees from selecting union representation, can be substantial. The law provides employers a great deal of leeway in campaigning against unionization. The low cost of remedies can serve to encourage employers who are so inclined to push their behavior to the outer edges of the law, knowing that the cost of falling over the edge is minimal.

Given this incentive structure in the Act, it is not surprising that some employers are extremely aggressive in resisting unionization. One women testified that she was fired by her employer, a large retail organization in New England, on the day after Thanksgiving, 1993.[10] The employee testified that prior to her discharge, her employer engaged in such activities as having her followed by security guards with walkie talkies when she went to restaurants on her day off, assigning a management person to watch her eight hours per day while at work, and timing her while she went to the restroom. She testified that it was "harassment beyond what I could ever tell you. Unless you have lived through it, you couldn't know what it feels like."[11]

An official of the Amalgamated Clothing and Textile Workers Union (ACTWU) and an employee testified about a firm that manufactures plastic components.[12] It employs approximately fifty people. According to the testimony, in 1993, some employees contacted the ACTWU about representation. In May 1993, the ACTWU had obtained authorization card signatures of thirty-three employees of a unit of forty-five. On May 25, the ACTWU petitioned for a representation election, which was eventually set for late July. The ACTWU official testified that after the election was set, the company began an antiunion campaign. The company's legal representatives were on site constantly. The company delivered captive audience speeches,[13] both department-wide and individually. Employees to whom management had never previously spoken were all contacted individually by the company in an attempt to change their minds about the union. The union still won the election by one vote.

The company, however, challenged the results of the election. There was a hearing on the challenge in September 1993, and the results were upheld in November 1993. On the day before Thanksgiving, however, the company discharged the employee who testified at the hearing.

A third firm was the subject of testimony from an ACTWU vice-president and an ACTWU organizer.[14] According to the testimony of these two individuals, the ACTWU was involved in an organizing campaign among 600 workers in a hosiery plant in a southern state. The company delivered captive audience speeches, made threats to close the plant, and took an amount of money equal to one year of dues from one paycheck. The company permitted an antiunion committee to have the run of the plant during working hours, while union supporters were required to stay on the job. The company organized the local bankers, while the union received support from local ministers.

Initially, 81 percent of the employees signed authorization cards. In an election held on July 22, 1993, the employees chose representation by a vote of 270-237. The company objected to the election. In January 1994, the NLRB dismissed the company's objections. While the objection proceedings were ongoing, three union supporters were discharged.

The same ACTWU official and a former employee described the situation at a textile manufacturer in the South.[15] In April and May of 1990, the workers overwhelmingly signed ACTWU authorization cards, and a union election was scheduled. The company immediately discharged the employee and her husband. The employee believed the purpose of the discharge was to frighten other workers, an effective tactic as there are few jobs in the small town in which the plant is located.

The union lost the election but filed unfair labor practice charges. The Board ultimately found the employer in violation of the Act, but the decision was not affirmed by the court of appeals until January 1993.

The NLRB ordered a new election to be held in April of 1993. In addition, the employee and her husband were reinstated with back pay. As of January 1994, however, they had not received their back pay. Meanwhile, another worker was discharged, and the employee and her husband were discharged for a second time in August 1993. She testified that the company had told the employees that they had no right to have a union at that firm. Her husband testified that the employees were told that the only right the employees had was "to go out the door."

A fifth firm was described by the organizing director of the Industrial Union Department of the AFL-CIO and a former employee of that firm.[16] The employee testified that she worked at the firm until September 29, 1993, when she was discharged. Discussions about unionization had begun in July 1993 and she was actively in favor of the union. She claimed that the company tried to intimidate employees by showing antiunion films and distributing antiunion pamphlets. She testified that "scare tactics" were used every day, as supervisors asked people how they were voting in the upcoming representation election.

The company initiated roundtable discussions at which only people opposed to unionization were allowed to speak. The employees were told that if the union won, the plant would close. The company had the president of the local Chamber of Commerce, school teachers, and a local minister speak to the employees. The testifying employee claimed her termination occurred when she received permission to go home because she felt sick in the morning; the company claimed she had walked out. She voted in the election, and the union needed that vote to win. The company objected to the election. Meanwhile, the NLRB issued a complaint on the employee's behalf.[17]

An international representative of the United Auto Workers and an employee testified about the situation in a supplier for the cosmetics industry located in the northeast.[18] In December 1992, the UAW representative had a meeting with a group of employees from the firm. On January 25, 1993, five employees signed authorization cards and became an organizing committee. The employees and the UAW representative began leafletting on February 3, 1993. During February, the union obtained authorization from sixty-two employees. According to the UAW representative, the labor law violations began on February 9, when a supervisor distributed a leaflet threatening the employees with loss of employment if they selected a union.

A consultant brought in by the company formed Spokespersons, an in-plant committee. The company posted notices for an election for Spokesperson officers and supervised the election on company time. The company discussed with Spokespersons such items as wages, benefits, and breaks.

On March 3, 1993, the UAW held a meeting. In attendance were three UAW in-plant organizing committee members. These three employees distributed union literature at the gates prior to start of shift and on breaks. After this distribution, the consultant threatened to close the plant. The consultant also informed employees that the company could say "no, no" in bargaining, and that selecting the union would be futile. The company also promised benefits, interrogated employees, and disciplined two union supporters.

On March 2, March 11, and March 17, the company warned, suspended, and again warned one of the in-plant committee members.

Also in March, the company prohibited employees from talking about unions on their facilities. On April 29, the company fired one employee, and on June 4, the company discharged two more union supporters.

One employee testified that his girlfriend had been fired. She has been out of work since April 1993. (The hearing at which the employee testified was held in January of 1994). The company has threatened to move, and they have instilled fear.

Based upon charges filed by the union, fourteen complaints were issued on August 4, 1993. As of January 5, 1994, the case was still awaiting a hearing.

Finally, there was much testimony about the situation in the health care sector in a large city in a border state.[19] One person who testified, a registered nurse representing an affiliate of the American Federation of State, County, and Municipal Employees, was involved in an organizing campaign at a large hospital (Hospital 1). She stated that two prounion nurses were "blacklisted" by hospitals in the city. One of the nurses was denied transfer to that hospital from a second hospital (Hospital 2). Instead, the position, one of two at Hospital 2, was awarded to a less-experienced, less-qualified nurse. It was also testified that two charge nurses at Hospital 1 who were union activists were removed from their positions and forced to reapply for those positions. One of the charge nurses who had fourteen years with the hospital was replaced by someone with only one year with the hospital.

Another registered nurse testified that she graduated from the local university in 1988 with a BS in Nursing. In June 1988, she was hired at Hospital 1. She became active in trying to organize a union, obtaining authorization card signatures of a majority of nurses in her unit. She was featured with other union leaders in a newspaper article.

In August 1989, she and a friend resigned their positions with Hospital 1 due to understaffing. There was a local nursing shortage at the time, and all local hospitals were trying to recruit nurses. They applied to a third hospital (Hospital 3), were interviewed, and told to report for work in the transitional care unit (TCU) at Hospital 3 on September 25, 1989.

On September 20, she and her friend received letters informing them that there was no position of employment for them at Hospital 3. In order to investigate the matter, another nurse who did not otherwise identify herself called Hospital 3 and inquired about a position in TCU at Hospital 3. It was testified that the nurse who called was told that the hospital had such positions. It was also testified that Hospital 3 had placed an advertisement in the newspaper of September 26, 1989 stating that it had positions in TCU.

The employee who claimed she was blacklisted testified that while she was at Hospital 1, she had excellent evaluations. Her overall average evaluations were 3.6, where 3.0 is satisfactory and 4.0 is excellent. She testified that she had a 5.0 in one area. She believes she was blacklisted for her union activity, and that this blacklisting created fear. She is now working as a nurse at a less satisfactory job.

Another person who testified worked in employee relations with the group that controlled two of the hospitals. His dates of employment were January 1989 to August 1992, at which time he was laid off. This person transferred into employee relations at Hospital 1 when it was facing a serious organizing campaign. He testified that the controlling organization was "vehemently antiunion" and that 80 percent of the time in employee relations was spent on antiunion activity. He testified that the organization was not concerned about the NLRB, and he had heard senior managers brag about their ability to defeat unions through illegal action. He said that the company collected personal information, correct or not, in order to prevent unionization—that the information could be used against somebody, or could be used to determine how they might vote in an organizing campaign. Moreover, this information was shared with other hospitals inside and outside the chain. He testified that he was in the office when the personnel director of Hospital 1 recommended to the personnel director of Hospital 3 that the employee and her friend not be hired.

An international representative from the ACTWU and two discharged workers testified about a foreign-owned firm based in Ohio.[20] One of the employees who testified was a member of a group that met with the ACTWU international representative and then told their supervisor they intended to organize a union. Soon after they informed their supervisor of this, all five employees were discharged for falsifying time sheets, despite the fact that the activity for which they were fired had been going on for years. The company also made personal attacks on the five discharged employees, spreading false claims that one was an alcoholic and that another was sexually harassing women. The workers were discharged on December 15, 1992, and charges were filed with the NLRB on December 17. A complaint was issued on February 27, 1993, and a hearing date was set for July 27 of that year. In March, the company asked for a postponement until August, and its request was granted. As of October 1993, the case had not been decided.

Meanwhile, the union obtained the signatures of a majority of the employees and petitioned for an election; an election was set for February 1993. The employer used captive audience speeches. The company also held meetings from which union supporters were banned and screened a film about an old strike involving the use of violence. The company hung newspaper articles on the bulletin boards about closed plants, pointing out that those could be pictures of their plant. They said that bargaining would "start from scratch" and that the workers could lose what they had. The campaigning went on every day for eight hours per day, including two-on-one meetings with workers during the last week of the campaign. Eventually, the union lost the election by a vote of 25-16.

An officer of United Food and Commercial Workers Local 951 described the attempts of workers to organize at a food retailer.[21] These attempts began in 1987. According to the testimony, the employer used professional management consultants. The union lost by a narrow margin and filed unfair labor practice charges and postelection objections. They stated that the employer put people in back rooms and questioned them about their union propensities in the presence of supervisors; no witnesses were present. The employer conducted surveillance of employees in and away from the workplace. The employer promised benefits if the union "went away" and threatened to close if it did not. There were also threats to discontinue benefits and job protection. Although the union prevailed in its charges, the Board proceedings lasted two years. The NLRB was ultimately upheld in the court of appeals, but no money had been paid to the employees as of October 13, 1993.

The president of Service Employees International Union Local 1199 described the situation at a nursing home owned by an organization that operates nursing homes throughout the United States.[22] An employee was suspended for asking a question during a captive audience speech, and a second worker was fired for accompanying the first to the office on her own time, while the suspension was taking place.

An official of the Kentucky State AFL-CIO described an organizing campaign at a meat processor in Kentucky.[23] In that case, the NLRB finally certified the election two years after election was held; the margin of victory was the votes of three illegally discharged employees. The employer has stated it will appeal the case.

Analysis. It is not the purpose of this monograph to determine the legality of these actions. Indeed, it is often difficult to distinguish between those activities that are technically legal and those that cross the line of illegality. That line is an extremely fine one.

What is clear is that even legal activities have the effect of infringing on the employee's right to choose. While it may be legal for several management personnel to call a single employee into an office and present to that employee the employer's view on unionization, the mere fact that an employee is in a room with several management personnel in an adversarial situation is likely to cause an employee to fear for his or her job if he/she chooses to vote against management's preference in a representation election.

A number of discharges associated with organizing campaigns were cited, as were other kinds of lesser workplace actions that could be construed as harassment for union activities. Whether those discharges and these lesser workplace actions were in violation of the law is less important than the fact that they seem to be an accepted method of resisting unions. These employers must be aware that discharge and discrimination in terms and conditions of employment for the purpose of discouraging union activity is unlawful. In view of the fact that an organizing campaign was in process when the discharges occurred, it is reasonable to believe that the employer had to have considered the possibility that its actions were unlawful. It appears they believed that the benefits, in terms of discouragement of union activity were worth the risk of a finding of a violation. Thus, it is clear that the law has done nothing to discourage aggressive employer behavior that, at best, is on the margin of legality, and at worst is illegal.

These situations result from the employer's control of the workplace. In essence, the employer can act, and any attempt to prevent the employer from acting as it wishes will meet with resistance through the legal process.

The delays in the processing of cases clearly injure employees. While the legal process continues, the employee continues to suffer without employment. In essence, the employer is able to shift to the employee the burden of determining the legality of the employer's actions.

Employer Behavior in Collective Bargaining

In addition to the right of self-organization, the law places on the employer the obligation to bargain with the union that the employees have chosen to represent them, should the employees so choose. As noted, the obligation to bargain with the employees' chosen representative is a natural extension of the right of the employees to choose a union to represent them. The right to select representation without a commensurate obligation on the employer to recognize and bargain with the union would make the right to choose a hollow right.

The law, however, also permits employers and unions to refuse to agree to anything. Good faith bargaining, under the law, requires only that the parties meet at reasonable times, consider issues relating to terms and conditions of employment, and to be willing to sign a contract. On the other hand, it does not require the making of a concession. At impasse, defined as the inability to come to agreement after good faith bargaining, the parties may use their economic weapons. The union may strike and the employer may implement its offer, lock the employees out and utilize temporary replacements, or both. If the union strikes, the employer may hire permanent replacements for the strikers at the terms and conditions in the employer's last proposal at impasse, provided strikers are permitted to return at any time during the strike if their jobs have not yet been filled.

Under the NLRA, then, reasoned bargaining, adherence to a position, the use of economic force, and self-help to offset the other party's of weapons are permitted. How this plays out in practice vis-a-vis the rights of employees who have chosen representation can be determined from Dunlop Commission testimony.

An official of Laborers Local 576 in Louisville and a former employee testified about the situation regarding a supplier of packaging materials to appliance manufacturers.[24] The union lost its first election among the employees of the firm in 1991, and attributed the loss to a company promise of wage increases. At the time, the employees were making $4.70 per hour. In a second election in November 1992, the employees chose representation. In June 1993, half of the employees struck after the company would not compromise on any proposal. The company then replaced the striking workers, including the employee who testified.[25]

An employee of a food processing firm in eastern Michigan testified but declined to identify himself for fear of employer retribution.[26] The employee was a member of the bargaining committee of a union certified to represent the employees of the firm. Although the union won the election in April 1992, it took an additional year for the union to be certified. He said that the company does not wish to bargain, and that they have withheld a wage increase. They came to the table only after the union filed charges. He said the company would not discuss safety issues, discharged people for being "discourteous" to supervisors, refused to consider the union's health care plan, and proposed an indefinite extension of the probationary period. He said the union has conceded to "a lot," and the employees do not want to strike; they need their jobs.

An official of the United Electrical Workers Union read a statement of an employee of a firm at which the union represented the employees.[27] According to the statement, the union attempted to negotiate a contract for fifteen months. The company, however, refused to recognize stewards for grievance handling purposes. Former union activists were fired. The union went out on an unfair labor practice strike on September 9, 1989. An unfair labor practice charge was filed, and in January 1991, an administrative law judge recommended a finding of a violation. The employees eventually went back to work in February 1991. In March, the union filed additional unfair labor practice charges against the company for refusing to bargain, discharging additional union-supporting employees, and illegally forcing workers to pay part of dental benefits. In April 1992, there was an additional unfair labor practice when the company unilaterally removed dental benefits. Following this, the company required employees who wished dental coverage to come to the office and sign an agreement saying they would agree not to file any labor board charges. Eventually, a court injunction was issued against the employer. Although a new company attorney has agreed to recognize stewards, the employees were still without an agreement as of January 1994.

A business representative of the International Brotherhood of Electrical Workers (IBEW) testified regarding a unit of IBEW-represented employees working for private contractors at an Air Force satellite station on the West Coast.[28] There were fifty-two employees in the bargaining unit, most of whom had been employed there for years. The various companies who had received the contract had always been unionized. In early 1992, a new firm obtained the Air Force contract and aggressively asserted management prerogatives. During that eighteen-month period, the firm lost fifteen arbitration cases heard under the existing collective agreement. In August 1993, negotiations opened for a new contract. The company came to the table with fifty-two proposals while the union had only nine. At the beginning of negotiations, the company said the union must accept seven proposals before any others could be discussed, and these proposals called for reductions in benefits. At the expiration of the contract on October 1, the company implemented all fifty-two proposals. The employees kept working and filed charges with the NLRB. The union requested mediation but the company refused. The union struck on October 11, 1993. On October 12, the company replaced all the workers. As all of the workers needed new security clearances, these costs were borne by the public. The union pointed out that the company was determined not to have violated the law by its actions.

Analysis. The foregoing cases indicate the impact of the NLRA philosophy of noninvolvement in the substance of bargaining. In theory, such a principle makes sense; one does not wish the government telling the parties to collective bargaining what to include in their collective agreements.

The noninvolvement principle does not operate in a vacuum, however. Rather, it can be combined with the property rights of the employer and the use of legal procedures under the NLRA to actually discourage true bargaining from occurring. Behaviors that can be used in organizing to discourage unionism can also be used to avoid coming to an agreement, with a result that the employee choice to bargain is frustrated after, rather than before, the choice is made.

Employers who are so inclined can behave like the Air Force contractor, which followed a very straightforward and simple strategy in

eliminating the union. First, the employer presents the union with proposals that it knows are unacceptable to it. As the government will not
become involved in the substance of proposals, this is not unlawful.
Second, the employer continues to meet at appropriate times. This sat-
isfies an important legal requirement. Third, the employer refuses to
compromise. This is legal, as the law does not require either party to
agree to anything or to make a concession.

At this point, the union usually chooses one of two options. It may
strike and risk replacement, or it may sign a contract it deems unacceptable. Either way the employer's strategy has been a success. In this
scenario, the employer has acted perfectly legally, but the union's
power is removed either under the threat of the company hiring
replacements or by the company carrying out that threat.

Conclusions

The NLRA, as amended and interpreted, permits behavior such as
was described in this chapter to occur at U.S. workplaces. The use of
legalism by employers, and the persistent exercise of procedural rights
to object to an election, to go to a hearing, or to appeal the decision of
an administrative law judge or the NLRB also have the effect of preventing employees from exercising their right to choose under the Act.

While there is no contention in this volume that all employers use
the law in this way, there is no doubt that the law can be used in this
way, and some employers take advantage of the law to the detriment of
their employees' rights. In this sense, we are aware that this chapter
may not present a complete picture of union organizing. These may
represent extreme examples; the majority of organizing campaigns
may not be associated with such behavior. But the fact that such behavior can and does occur is, in our judgement, sufficient to take notice. If
behavior is undesirable, it does not become less so because only a
minority of persons engage in it.

One point seems particularly relevant. Although the employer may
act legally, the result of pyramiding legal activities one on top of
another is an outcome that was surely not intended by the Act. The
NLRA was enacted to provide employees with a free and uncoerced

choice regarding whether to be represented by a union and to provide the employees in a unit in which a union was chosen the right to bargain collectively. The law can be used, however, to achieve precisely the opposite result.

Two examples will illustrate the point. The employer may exercise its legal rights under the NLRA to speak to employees about unionization, its control over its employees' time to require the employees to hear the employer's message during working hours, its control over its employees' time to limit the employees' ability to discuss unionization during working hours, and, its control over its property to prevent the union from entering the property. While the exercise of each of these rights may be justifiable by themselves, taken together they result in a substantial imbalance in favor of the employer in the ability of the employee to receive information about unionization. Moreover, taken together, they provide a demonstration of the employer's power over the employee, making the choice of unionization appear much more costly to the employees than it might otherwise be perceived.

A second example is in the bargaining context. An employer, by exercising a legal right to make a proposal that is unacceptable to the union and its legal right to refuse to make a concession, and by pointing out its option to replace striking workers, can place the union in a position in which it must accept what the employer proposes or strike and risk replacement. In the first instance, the employees choice to bargain collectively has been frustrated because no true "give-and-take" bargaining has occurred. In the second instance, employees have lost their jobs because they chose to unionize and bargain collectively.

Unfortunately, the Board seems to have no vehicle for making a finding of an unfair labor practice based on the results of a series of otherwise lawful acts. Under our legal system, each allegation is examined discretely, and a decision is made based on that allegation. Although there is a long-established doctrine under the NLRA under which the Board can examine the "totality of conduct" on the part of the employer to establish "hostile motive" for alleged discrimination to discourage union membership, this doctrine is triggered only when there is an allegation of an illegal action.

A second issue is the ability of the employer to use its procedural rights to resist unionization. The employer may exercise its due process rights to appeal adverse Board rulings, and then exercise its management and property rights to require employees to bear the burden of the delay associated with the employer's exercise of its due process rights, possibly through a lost job or an inability to obtain a contract.

The implications of this will be discussed in the concluding chapter.

NOTES

1. It has been argued that this provision impairs employers' ability to create employee participation structures where no union exists.

2. A greater appreciation of the principle of unit determination can be obtained by examining the wording of Section 9(b):

> The Board shall decide in each case whether in order to assure to employees the fullest freedom of association in exercising the rights guaranteed by this Act, the unit appropriate for the purposes of collective bargaining shall be the employer unit, craft unit, plant unit, or subdivision thereof.

3. See, for example, Roomkin and Block (1981).

4. Although the benefits and costs of unionization for any particular group of employees cannot be fully discussed here, a short summary might be useful. In general, union representation means that employees may not negotiate with their employer individually for terms and conditions of employment that differ from those bargained for the entire unit. The major benefits of unionization lie in the hope that a union will be able to obtain better terms and conditions of employment, on average, by negotiating collectively than the employee will be able to obtain individually and to create objective, enforceable standards for employer decision making vis-a-vis employees.

5. An item in the "Work Week" column of *The Wall Street Journal* for November 15, 1994 (page 1) will illustrate the point. The item is quoted in full:

> *Ten years after charges of unfair labor practices, workers collect $16 million.*
> Donald Griffin, 47, was president of Allied Industrial Workers Local 879 in 1984 when U.S. Marine Co. bought a Hartford, Wis. boat engine factory from Chrysler Corp. and clashed with the union. Today, former coworkers give him much of the credit for the back pay settlement due 620 workers from U.S. Marine's successor, Brunswick Corp.
>
> Mr. Griffin says 17 of the 262 workers who originally started the case are dead. Of the 34 workers who the National Labor Relations Board says weren't rehired for antiunion reasons, two lost their homes because they couldn't meet the mortgage payments. Mr. Griffin, who pursued the case from his basement during off hours, says the stress played a part in the breakup of his first marriage. With seemingly endless appeals, it became a test of "who can hold out the longest."
>
> Brunswick says the case could have gone on to the year 2000, and it made a "business decision" to settle now (italics in original).

6. Kleiner has argued that the sanctions against employers for violating the NLRA are not sufficient to deter employers who are so inclined from violating the Act. Put differently, Kleiner found that the benefits, in terms of lower costs of operation without a union and the increased probability of preventing unionization far outweigh any costs associated with the remedial structure of the Act. The conclusion then, was that the incentive structure in the law encouraged violations of the law. See Kleiner (1984, 1994).

7. For the legal doctrine, see, for example, *H.K. Porter Co. v. NLRB*, 397 U.S. 99 (1970).

8. For the governing legal doctrine, see, for example, *NLRB* v. *Mackay Radio and Telegraph Co.*, 304 U.S. 333 (1938); *NLRB* v. *Insurance Agents International Union*, 361 U.S. 477 (1960); and *American Ship Building Co.* v. *NLRB*, 380 U.S. 300 (1965).

9. All cases were found in the *Labor Relations Reference Manual* published by the Bureau of National Affairs. LRRM is available at the Labor and Industrial Relations Library at Michigan State University and at most law libraries in the United States. Cites for these cases have been omitted to protect the names of these firms from being widely disseminated. The cites are available from the authors upon request.

10. *Transcript of the Hearing of the Commission on the Future of Worker-Management Relations*, Boston, Massachusetts, January 5, 1994, pp. 66, 195-97.

11. *Transcript of the Hearing of the Commission on the Future of Worker-Management Relations*, Boston, Massachusetts, January 5, 1994, p.196.

12. *Transcript of the Hearing of the Commission on the Future of Worker-Management Relations*, Boston, Massachusetts, January 5, 1994, pp. 161-67.

13. A "captive audience" speech is delivered when the employer directs one or more employees to hear the employer's message. The employees do not have the option of leaving the room or otherwise not listening to the message. For an employee to decline to expose him- or herself to the message would be insubordination.

14. *Transcript of the Hearing of the Commission on the Future of Worker-Management Relations*, Atlanta, Georgia, January 11, 1994, pp. 149-55.

15. *Transcript of the Hearing of the Commission on the Future of Worker-Management Relations*, Atlanta, Georgia, January 11, 1994, pp. 1588-62.

16. *Transcript of the Hearing of the Commission on the Future of Worker-Management Relations*, Atlanta, Georgia, January 11, 1994, pp. 130-35.

17. Under Board procedure, its regional office, on behalf of the Board's General Counsel, issues a "complaint," when, after investigation of a charge, it has reasonable cause to believe a violation of the NLRA occurred.

18. *Transcript of the Hearing of the Commission on the Future of Worker-Management Relations*, Boston, Massachusetts, January 5, 1994, pp. 138-52.

19. *Transcript of the Hearing of the Commission on the Future of Worker-Management Relations*, Louisville, Kentucky, September 22, 1993, pp. 229-44.

20. *Transcript of the Hearing of the Commission on the Future of Worker-Management Relations*, East Lansing, Michigan, October 13, 1993, pp. 158-69.

21. *Transcript of the Hearing of the Commission on the Future of Worker-Management Relations, East* Lansing, Michigan, October 13, 1993, pp. 170-76. See also 300 N.L.R.B. 649, 136 LRRM 1212 (1990).

22. *Transcript of the Hearing of the Commission on the Future of Worker-Management Relations,* East Lansing, Michigan, October 13, 1993, pp. 187-94. A quote from the Board decision in the case is instructive:

> This consolidated case concerns violations which occurred primarily during a 2-year period from the summer of 1986 through the spring of 1988. During that period the (firm) committed some 135 unfair labor practices at 32 of the 35 facilities here at issue. . . .

> We find . . . that the (firm) has demonstrated a proclivity to violate the act . . . .. (cite available on request

23. *Transcript of the Hearing of the Commission on the Future of Worker-Management Relations,* Louisville, Kentucky, September 22, 1993, pp. 212-15. See also 145 LRRM 1144 (August

10, 1993), 145 LRRM 1280 (January 31, 1994). The latter decision was reported by the BNA as follows:

> . . . the employer was found to have violated (the NLRA) by refusing to bargain with a newly certified union. In a ruling on a motion for summary judgement, the NLRB found that all representation issues raises were, or could have been, litigated in a prior representation proceeding, that the employer did not offer a newly discovered, previously unavailable evidence, and that it did not show any special circumstances required the board to reexamine the decision made in the representation proceeding (145 LRRM at 1280).

24. *Transcript of the Hearing of the Commission on the Future of Worker-Management Relations,* Louisville, Kentucky, October 22, 1993, pp. 253-59.

25. The charge of the Commission on the Future of Worker-Management Relations excluded matters involving the permanent replacement of economic strikers because a bill prohibiting permanent replacements was being considered in Congress at the time of the hearings. Thus, the Commission did not seek such testimony, and there was very little such testimony at the hearings. Some testimony on permanent replacements was occasionally offered, however, at the initiative of those appearing before the Commission, in the context of other matters within the charge of the Commission.

26. *Transcript of the Hearing of the Commission on the Future of Worker-Management Relations,* East Lansing, Michigan, October 13, 1994, pp. 181-87.

27. *Transcript of the Hearing of the Commission on the Future of Worker-Management Relations,* Boston, Massachusetts, January 5, 1994, pp. 88-97. See also 142 LRRM 1308 (September 30, 1992), 143 LRRM 1204 (December 16, 1992).

28. *Transcript of the Hearing of the Commission on the Future of Worker-Management Relations,* San Jose, California, January 27, 1994, pp. 330-35.

CHAPTER 5

Summary and Conclusions

The purpose of this volume has been to use the testimony before the Commission on the Future of Worker-Management Relations to gain insight into the state of industrial relations and labor law in the United States in the mid-1990s. To that end, chapter 2 explored in some detail the evolution of labor law since 1935, changes in industrial relations practice associated with that evolution, and changes in the economic environment. Both the unionized and the emergent nonunion systems were analyzed. The lesson from chapter 2 was that the essence of the National Labor Relations Act is employee choice in the matter of union representation. Labor law was designed to create a system by which employees could exercise a choice to select, or to reject, union representation. If the employees chose union representation, the law was designed to provide them with the fruits of that choice by obligating the employer to negotiate with their chosen representative.

This ideal, however, is not always met. Because U.S. labor policy is based on the principle of governmental noninvolvement in the bargaining process, and because of the characteristics of processing and deciding both representation and unfair labor practice cases under the NLRA, our industrial relations system manifests wide variation in the extent to which the principle of employee choice is honored in actual practice.

Chapter 3 provided examples of firms that respect the right of employee choice. Unionized firms profiled in that chapter engaged in extensive cooperation and innovative relationships with the unions representing their employees, often bringing in the union as a partner in making important decisions. On occasion, such a relationship was facilitated by governmental structures. For example, the governmental agencies in the metropolitan area around Louisville, Kentucky supported labor-management cooperation. Bargaining relationships that have benefited include those between Philip Morris and the Bakery, Confectionery, and Tobacco Workers Union, and between Louisville Gas and Electric and the International Brotherhood of Electrical Workers.

The Federal Mediation and Conciliation Service has also been active in encouraging parties to improve their relationships, expanding its role beyond the traditional one of helping to resolve labor disputes. The result is that disputes are avoided. Examples of relationships that have benefited from FMCS involvement are that between Reynolds Metals Corporation and the International Association of Machinists and between Healthspan Corporation (of Minneapolis/St. Paul) and the Service Employees International Union.

A key to respecting employee choice under the National Labor Relations Act appears to be the willingness of the parties to avoid legalism, to minimize insistence on exploring and exercising legal rights vis-a-vis the other party. The parties in innovative and cooperative relationships such as those highlighted in chapter 3 directly interact with each other based on their respective interests. They negotiate a resolution of their problems on a face-to-face basis, as issues arise. They eschew an adversarial relationship through the NLRB and the courts. Examples of this type of relationship are the Ford Motor Company and the United Auto Workers, New United Manufacturing Company and the UAW, Miller Brewing and the UAW, and National Steel and the United Steelworkers of America.

As labor law in the United States is designed to provide employees with a choice regarding whether they wish a union to represent them, it is not surprising that many employees are not represented by a union. Indeed, a major phenomenon in industrial relations in the last quarter century has been the development of employee relations systems for nonunion employees. Many nonunion or partially unionized firms have adopted employee relations practices that create objective or merit-based systems for making decisions regarding employee relations issues. Such firms often view their employees as assets to be utilized rather than as costs to be minimized. These firms often create programs that encourage employee involvement in the production process. Examples of such firms include Texas Instruments, Coca-Cola, Delta Airlines, Herman Miller, and Donnelly Corporation.

Although the employees in such firms have not necessarily ever made an explicit choice against union representation, there is no reason to believe that there is a broad-based desire on the part of employees in these firms for collective bargaining. Such firms develop strong employment relations systems so that the matter of alternative employee choices is seldom an issue. Broad-based employee disinterest in unionism and the absence of widespread employee quitting suggests that, while these employees have not made an explicit choice against union representation, it is likely that they would decline such representation if asked. This, in essence, is a form of employee choice against union representation, and it is perfectly legal and proper. The only other policy option is to assert that employers may not voluntarily treat their employees well, because to do so denies the employees the opportunity to choose. This, it seems, is an untenable position to take.

By comparison, other firms avoid unionization by striking fear among employees who attempt to unionize. Such firms use aspects of the legal process to overtly resist the unionization of their employees. They use the right to object to the proposed bargaining unit and to refuse to agree to other stipulations to gain time to campaign against union representation. They may threaten, coerce, or even discharge employees, knowing that the penalties for such illegal behavior can be delayed for months, through appeals of NLRB decisions. Moreover, the remedies, when and if imposed, are weak. Indeed, it is likely that the cost of an unfair labor practice is far less than the cost of a union, suggesting a system that encourages labor law violations rather than labor law compliance.

If the employees ultimately choose representation, the legal system permits employers to resist the choice by creating an incentive to refuse to bargain collectively, knowing that the only remedy available to the Board is a cease-and-desist order. The use of self-help, combined with governmental noninvolvement in the bargaining process, permits an employer to maintain a position that is unacceptable to the union, knowing that the union must risk permanent replacement of its members if it strikes. Should permanent replacement occur, an attempt to decertify the union is the final step. In essence, the pyramiding of legal rights gives the employer the means to legally rid itself of a union chosen by the employees, a result that was surely not contemplated by the drafters of the National Labor Relations Act.

It is outside the scope of this volume to present policy recommendations. The final report of the Commission on the Future of Worker-Management Relations has advocated some changes in the nation's labor laws.[1] Such recommendations have been made in other places as well.[2]

What is clear from the hearings, however, is that labor law in the United States permits great variation in the extent to which employers respect the mechanism by which workers make a choice for or against union representation and the rights of employees who choose union representation to have that choice honored. While some employers honor that choice, other employers do not. While the law applauds the former, it cannot seem to prevent the latter. Ironically, then, a system that was designed to provide a choice of representation to *employees* seems only to provide *employers* with a choice—a choice as to the type of employee relations system they will create.

Such a system, we submit, must be changed. It is our view that the law should reaffirm the rights of employees to make a choice for or against union representation, and changes to the election and bargaining process are needed to facilitate the choice. While employers should be able to participate in that process, the law should provide for the involvement of the union in that process as well, so that employees hear both views with equal clarity. The labor law remedial structure should be closely examined to insure that law-abiding employers do not perceive themselves as being placed at a competitive disadvantage by their counterparts who may wish to engage in legal brinkmanship. The law should explicitly state a preference for employee relations to be administered through cooperation rather than through conflict.

A final issue is the matter of the pyramiding of legal rights to create a result that, while not illegal, is clearly inconsistent with the principles of the National Labor Relations Act. Thus, an important policy implication is the need to empower the Board to address conduct which, while not illegal in any of the particulars, has the overall effect of interfering with employee choice.

While there are certainly numerous policy suggestions that can be made, perhaps the best answer was given by Peter Pestillo of Ford, who pointed out that the law plays but a negligible role in the relationship between Ford and the UAW. This suggests that the labor law that works best may be the law that is invoked the least, that creates a system to encourage the parties to resolve their disputes through respect for employee choice. The hearings and this volume have illustrated the costs of failure to honor employee choice through overreliance on the law. Thus, the best answer may be less reliance on the law and legal processes.

What is clear is that many employers and employees have been supported by cooperative systems, and that many employees have been hurt by conflict and the failure to recognize the legitimacy of employee rights to choose. A full recognition of the benefits of respecting employee choice, and the costs of impairing it, is the first step toward change.

NOTES

1. See Commission on the Future of Worker-Management Relations, *Report and Recommendations* (1994).

2. See, for example, most recently, Gould (1993); and Friedman, Hurd, Oswald, and Seeber (1994).

References

Adams, George. 1994. *Canadian Labour Law*, 2nd edition. Aurora, Ontario: Canada Law Book.

Adams, Graham, Jr. 1966. *Age of Industrial Violence 1910-1915: The Activities and Findings of the United States Commission on Industrial Relations.* New York and London: Columbia University Press.

Adams, Roy J. 1981. "A Theory of Employer Attitudes and Behavior Towards Trade Unions in Western Europe and North America." In *Management Under Differing Value Systems: Political, Social, and Economic Perspectives in a Changing World*, Gunter Dlagos and Klaus Weiermair, eds. Berllin and New York: Walter de Gruyter.

Avery, Dianne. 1989. "Federal Labor Rights and Access to Private Property: the NLRB and the Right to Exclude," *Industrial Relations Law Journal* 11, 1: 145-227.

Barnett, Donald, and Louis Schorsch. 1984. *Steel: Upheaval in a Basic Industry.* Cambridge, MA: Ballinger.

Belzer, Michael. 1994. "The Motor Carrier Industry: Truckers and Teamsters Under Siege." In *Contemporary Collective Bargaining in the Private Sector*, Paula D. Voos, ed. Madison, WI: Industrial Relations Research Association.

Bernstein, Irving. 1969. *Turbulent Years: A History of the American Worker 1933-1941.* Boston: Houghton-Mifflin.

Block, Richard N. 1990a. "American Industrial Relations in the 1980s: Transformation or Evolution?" In *Reflections on the Transformation of Industrial Relations*, Institute of Management and Labor Relations Series No. 1, James Chelius and James Dworkin, eds. Metuchen, NJ: IMLR Press/Rutgers University.

_____. 1990b. "Redressing the Imbalance in the Law of Union Representation: The Principle of Workplace Neutrality," Industrial Relations Research Association Series, Proceedings of the 43rd Annual Meeting, Washington, D.C.

_____. 1993. "Employee Participation Plans and the NLRA: Toward Making (Some) Sense From *Electromation*," *Dialogues* 1, 1 (May): 1, 3.

_____. 1994. "Reforming U.S. Labor Law and Collective Bargaining: Some Proposals Based on the Canadian System." In *Restoring the Promise of American Labor Law*, S. Friedman, R. Hurd, R. Oswald, and R. Seeber, eds. Ithaca, NY: Cornell, ILR Press.

Block, Richard N., and Joel L. Cutcher-Gershenfeld. 1992. "Traditional and Nontraditional Systems of Resolving Disputes Under Collective Bargaining," *Workplace Topics* 2, 3 (July): 113-

Block, Richard N., Christine L. Mahoney, and Leslie F. Corbitt. 1987. "The Impact of Employment-at-Will Judicial Decisions on the Outcomes of NLRB Representation Elections," Proceedings of the 39th Annual Meeting of the Industrial Relations Research Association, New Orleans.

Block, Richard N., and Kenneth McLennan. 1985. "Structural Change and Industrial Relations in the United States' Manufacturing and Transportation Sectors: 1973- 1983." In *The Response of Industrial Relations to Economic Change*, Harvey Juris, Mark Thompson, and Wilbur Daniels, eds. Madison, WI: Industrial Relations Research Association.

Block, Richard N., and Steven L. Premack. 1983. "The Unionization Process: A Review of the Literature." In *Advances in Industrial and Labor Relations* vol. 1, David B. Lipsky and Joel M. Douglas, eds. Greenwich, CT: JAI Press. pp. 31-70.

Block, Richard N. and Myron Roomkin. 1995. "Observations on Legalism in Industrial Relations in the United States," paper presented at the 47th Annual Meeting of the Industrial Relations Research Association, Washington, D.C.

Block, Richard N., and Benjamin W. Wolkinson. 1986. "Delay in the Union Election Campaign Revisited: A Theoretical and Empirical Analysis." In *Advances in Industrial and Labor Relations*, vol. 3, David B. Lipsky and David Lewin, eds. Greenwich, CT: JAI Press.

_____. 1989. "Impediments to Innovative Employee Relations Arrangements," *Investing in People: A Strategy to Address America's Workforce Crisis*. U.S. Department of Labor, Commission on Workforce Quality and Labor Market Efficiency, September, pp. 1976-1991.

Block, Richard N., Benjamin W. Wolkinson, and James W. Kuhn. 1988. "Some Are More Equal Than Others: the Relative Status of Employers, Unions, and Employees in the Law of Union Organizing," *Industrial Relations Law Journal* 10, 2: 220-240.

Capelli, Peter. 1987. "Airlines." In *Collective Bargaining in American Industry: Contemporary Perspectives and Future Directions*, David B. Lipsky and Clifford Donn, eds. Lexington, MA: D.C. Heath.

Capelli, Peter, and Peter D. Sherer. 1990. "Assessing Worker Attitudes Under a Two-Tier Wage Plan,: *Industrial and Labor Relations Review* 43, 2 (January): 225-244.

Chaison, Gary N., and Joseph B. Rose. 1991. "Continental Divide: The Direction and Fate of North American Unions." In *Advances in Industrial and*

Labor Relations, Donna Sockell, David Lewin, and David B. Lipsky, eds. Greenwich, CT: JAI Press, pp. 160-205.

Commission on the Future of Worker-Management Relations. 1994a."Fact-Finding Report." U.S. Departments of Labor and Commerce.

_____. 1994b. "Report and Recommendations." U.S. Department of Labor and Commerce.

Cooke, William N. 1983. "Determinants of the Outcomes of Union Certification Elections," *Industrial and Labor Relations Review* 36, 3 (April): 402-412.

_____. 1985. "The Failure to Negotiate First Contracts: Determinants and Policy Implications," *Industrial and Labor Relations Review* 38, 2 (January): 163-178.

_____. 1990. *Labor-Management Cooperation: New Partnerships or Going in Circles?* Kalamazoo, MI: W.E. Upjohn Institute for Employment Research.

_____. 1992. "Product Quality Improvement Through Employee Participation: The Effects of Unionization and Joint Union-Management Administration," *Industrial and Labor Relations Review* 46, 1 (October): 119-134.

_____. 1994. "Employee Participation Programs, Group-Based Incentives, Company Performance: A Union-Nonunion Comparison,: *Industrial and Labor Relations Review* 47, 4 (July): 594-609.

Cutcher-Gershenfeld, Joel. 1991. "The Impact on Economic Performance of a Transformation in Workplace Relations," *Industrial and labor Relations Review* 44, 2 (January): 241-260.

Fillippelli, Ronald L. ed. 1990. *Labor Conflict in the United States: An Encyclopedia*. New York and London: Garland Publishers.

"Final Report and Testimony submitted to Congress by the Commission on Industrial Relations Created by the Act of August 23, 1912," vol. 1. 1916. Washington DC: Government Printing Office.

Freeman, Richard B., and James Medoff. 1984. *What Do Unions Do?* New York: Basic Books.

Friedman, S., R. Hurd, R. Oswald, and R. Seeber, eds. 1994. *Restoring the Promise of American Labor Law*. Ithaca, NY: ILR Press.

Gershenfeld, Walter J. 1987. "Employee Participation in Firm Decisions." In *Human Resources and the Performance of the Firm*, M. Kleiner, R. Block, M. Roomkin, and S. Salzburg, eds. Madison, WI: Industrial Relations Research Association.

Golden, Clinton S., and Virginia D. Parker, eds. 1955. *Causes of Industrial Peace Under Collective Bargaining*. New York: Harper.

Gould, William B., IV. 1993. *Agenda for Reform: The Future of Employment Relationships and the Law*. Cambridge, MA: MIT Press.

Hirsch, Barry T. 1991. *Labor Unions and the Economic Performance of Firms*. Kalamazoo, MI: W.E. Upjohn Institute for Employment Research.

Hoerr, John. 1988. *And the Wolf Finally Came: The Decline of the American Steel Industry*. Pittsburgh: University of Pittsburgh Press.

Katz, Harry C. 1985. *Shifting Gears: Changing Labor Relations in the U.S. Auto Industry*. Cambridge: MIT Press.

Katz, Harry C., and John Paul McDuffie. 1994. "Collective Bargaining in the U.S. Auto Assembly Sector." In *Contemporary Collective Bargaining in the Private Sector*, Paula D. Voos, ed. Madison, WI: Industrial Relations Research Association.

Karper, Mark D. 1987. "Tires." In *Collective Bargaining in American Industry*, David B. Lipsky and Clifford B Donn, eds. Lexington, MA: D.C. Heath.

Keyserling, Leon. 1945. "Why the Wagner Act?" In *The Wagner Act: After Ten Years*, Louis B. Silverbert, ed. Washington, DC: Bureau of National Affairs.

Kleiner, Morris M. 1984. "Unionism and Employer Discrimination: Analysis of 8(a)(3) Violations," *Industrial Relations* 23, 2 (spring): 234-243.

_____. 1994. "What Will It Take: Establishing the Economic Costs to Management of Noncompliance with the NLRA." In *Restoring the Promise of American Labor Law*, S. Friedman, R. Hurd, R. Oswald, and R. Seeber, eds. Ithaca, NY: ILR Press.

Kleiner, Morris M., Richard N. Block, Myron Roomkin, and Sidney Salsburg, eds. 1987. *Human Resources and the Performance of the Firm*. Madison, WI: Industrial Relations Research Association.

Kochan, Thomas A., Harry C. Katz, and Robert B. McKersie. 1994. *The Transformation of American Industrial Relations*. Ithaca, NY: ILR Press (originally published 1986).

Kochan, Thomas A., Harry C. Katz, and Nancy R. Mower. 1984. *Worker Participation and American Unions: Threat or Opportunity?* Kalamazoo, MI: W.E. Upjohn Institute for Employment Research.

Levine, David I., and Laura D'Andrea Tyson. 1990. "Participation and Productivity in the Firm's Environment." In *Paying for Productivity: A Look at the Evidence*, Alan S. Blinder, ed. Washington, DC: Brookings Institution.

Martin, James E., with Thomas D. Heetderks. 1990. *Two-Tier Compensation Structures: their Impact on Unions, Employers, and Employees*. Kalamazoo, MI: W.E. Upjohn Institute for Employment Research.

Meltz, Noah. 1990. "Unionism in Canada, U.S.: On Parallel Treadmills," *Forum for Applied Research and Public Policy* 15 (winter):46-52.

Millis, Harry, and Emily Clark Brown. 1950. *From the Wagner Act to Taft-Hartley: A Study of National Labor Policy.* Chicago: University of Chicago Press.

Nash, Peter G. 1985. "The NLRA at Age Fifty," Proceedings of the Spring Meeting, Industrial Relations Research Association, Detroit.

Neumann, George R., and Ellen Rissman. 1984. "Where Have All the Union Members Gone?" *Journal of Labor Economics* 2 (April): 175-192

Oberer, Walter E., Kurt L. Hanslowe, Jerry R. Anderson, and Timothy J. Heinsz. 1986. *Labor Law: Collective Bargaining in a Free Society,* 3rd edition. St. Paul, MN: West Publishing.

Oberer, Walter E., Kurt L. Hanslowe, and Timothy J. Heinsz. 1994. *Statutory Supplement to Cases and Materials on Labor Law: Collective Bargaining in a Free Society,* 4th edition. St. Paul, MN: West Publishing.

Organization for Economic Cooperation and Development (OECD). 1991. "Trends in Trade Union Membership," *OECD Outlook, 1991.* Paris: OECD.

Perlman, Selig. 1966. *A Theory of the Labor Movement.* New York: Augustus Kelley (originally published 1928).

Prosten, Richard. 1978. "The Longest Season: Union Organizing in the Last Decade, a/k/a How Come One Team Has to Play With Its Shoelaces Tied Together," Proceedings of the Thirty-first Annual Meeting of the Industrial Relations Research Association, Chicago.

Roomkin, Myron, and Richard N. Block. 1981. "Case Processing Time and the Outcomes of Representation Elections: Some Empirical Evidence," *University of Illinois Law Review* 1: 75-94

Sisson, Keith. 1987. *The Management of Collective Bargaining: An International Comparison.* Oxford, U.K.: Basil Blackwell.

Sockell, Donna. 1984. "The Legality of Employee participation Programs in Unionized Firms," *Industrial and Labor Relations Review* 37, 4 (July):

_____. 1986. "The Scope of Mandatory Bargaining: A Critique and a Proposal," *Industrial and Labor Relations Review* 40, 1 (October): 19-34.

Taylor, George W. 1948. *Government Regulation of Industrial Relations.* New York: Prentice-Hall.

"Termination Report of the National War Labor Board: Industrial Disputes During Wartime, January 12, 1942-December 31, 1945," vols. 1-3. 1946. Washington, DC: Government Printing Office.

Troy, Leo. 1965. "Trade Union Membership, 1897-1962." Occasional Paper No. 92, National Bureau of Economic Research.

U.S. Department of Labor, Bureau of Labor-Management Relations and Cooperative Programs. 1986, 1987. *U.S. Labor Law and the Future of Labor-Management Cooperation,* BLMR 104, BLMR 113.

Voos, Paula. 1987. "Managerial Perceptions of the Economic Impact of Labor Relations Programs," *Industrial and Labor Relations Review* 40, 2 (January): 195-208.

_____. 1994. "An Economic Perspective on Contemporary Trends in Collective Bargaining." In *Contemporary Collective Bargaining in the Private Sector*, Paula Voos, ed. Madison, WI: Industrial Relations Research Association.

Walton, Richard E., Joel Cutcher-Gershenfeld, and Robert B. McKersie. 1994. *Strategic Negotiations: A Theory of Change in Labor-Management Relations.* Boston: Harvard Business School Press.

Weiler, Paul. 1983. "Promises to Keep: Securing Workers' Rights to Self-Organization Under the NLRA," *Harvard Law Review* 96 (June): 1769-1827.

Witte, Edwin H. 1946. "Wartime Handling of Labor Disputes," *Harvard Business Review* 25: 169-89.

Index

About the Institute

The W.E. Upjohn Institute for Employment Research is a nonprofit research organization devoted to finding and promoting solutions to employment-related problems at the national, state, and local level. It is an activity of the W.E. Upjohn Unemployment Trustee Corporation, which was established in 1932 to administer a fund set aside by the late Dr. W.E. Upjohn, founder of The Upjohn Company, to seek ways to counteract the loss of employment income during economic downturns.

The Institute is funded largely by income from the W.E. Upjohn Unemployment Trust, supplemented by outside grants, contracts, and sales of publications. Activities of the Institute are comprised of the following elements: (1) a research program conducted by a resident staff of professional social scientists; (2) a competitive grant program, which expands and complements the internal research program by providing financial support to researchers outside the Institute; (3) a publications program, which provides the major vehicle for the dissemination of research by staff and grantees, as well as other selected work in the field; and (4) an Employment Management Services division, which manages most of the publicly funded employment and training programs in the local area.

The broad objectives of the Institute's research, grant, and publication programs are to: (1) promote scholarship and experimentation on issues of public and private employment and unemployment policy; and (2) make knowledge and scholarship relevant and useful to policymakers in their pursuit of solutions to employment and unemployment problems.

Current areas of concentration for these programs include: causes, consequences, and measures to alleviate unemployment; social insurance and income maintenance programs; compensation; workforce quality; work arrangements; family labor issues; labor-management relations; and regional economic development and local labor markets.